LET'S GET
dipping!

LET'S GET
dipping!

Over 80 easy & delicious recipes to whip up at home

RYLAND PETERS & SMALL
LONDON • NEW YORK

Designer Paul Stradling
Senior Editor Abi Waters
Head of Production Patricia Harrington
Creative Director Leslie Harrington
Editorial Director Julia Charles

Indexer Vanessa Bird

This edition published in 2024 by
Ryland Peters & Small
20–21 Jockey's Fields
London
WC1R 4BW
and
341 E 116th St
New York
NY 10029

www.rylandpeters.com

ISBN: 978-1-78879-604-0

A CIP record for this book is available from
the British Library.
US Library of Congress CIP data has been
applied for.

Printed in China

notes

• Both British (Metric) and American (Imperial plus US cup) measurements are included in these recipes for your convenience; however it is important to work with one set of measurements only and not alternate between the two within a recipe.

• All spoon measurements are level unless otherwise specified.

• All eggs are medium (UK) or large (US), unless otherwise specified. Uncooked or partially cooked eggs should not be served to the very old, frail, young children, pregnant women or those with compromised immune systems.

• When a recipe calls for the grated zest of citrus fruit, buy unwaxed fruit and wash well before using. If you can only find treated fruit, scrub well in warm soapy water before using.

• Ovens should be preheated to the specified temperatures. We recommend using an oven thermometer. If using a fan-assisted oven, adjust temperatures according to the manufacturer's instructions.

Contents

Introduction

Who doesn't enjoy a delicious dip? The ultimate in food for sharing, dips are most often enjoyed at social gatherings – from drinks or a movie night in with a few friends to celebratory parties and special occasion buffets. Designed to be enjoyed from a communal bowl, dips can be paired with dippers to create customized bites to suit every taste and are often eaten with one hand, leaving the other hand free to cope with a glass of wine! Here are some simple guidelines to successful dip service:

Season with care. Although it's usual to season to taste during preparation, it's best to check the seasoning of your dip with your intended dipper. Salted or peppered breadsticks or crackers may mean that less seasoning is required in the dip itself. Likewise if you are serving a dip with very bland dippers, the dip needs to be full of flavour and bordering on over-seasoned. A squeeze of lemon juice or a splash of wine vinegar can often give a dip the lift it needs at the last minute.

Allow time. Where possible avoid serving your dips straight from the fridge. Giving them a little time to come to room temperature will mean they are a better dipping consistency and have a fuller flavour. Hot dips should be served hot, of course, but not dangerously so. Always carefully check the temperature of a hot dip yourself before serving to others.

Presentation matters. Garnishing your dips creatively can make them more appealing as well as hint at the flavours contained within. Reserve a sprig of fresh herbs, a few jewel-bright edamame beans or pomegranate seeds; add a scattering of toasted pine nuts or sesame seeds; a dusting of paprika for colour contrast or a slick of good quality olive oil, balsamic glaze or pomegranate molasses can look very attractive. Always add your garnish just before serving.

Perfect pairings – which dippers to choose?

Crisps/chips Potato crisps/chips have a deliciously crunchy texture and are often quite resilient. Choose from the numerous potato, root vegetable, corn, rice, pitta or bagel products available in stores or make your own using the recipes provided in this book. Try and flavour-match your chips and dips sympathetically – for example, sweet potato chips work well with cool, creamy dips; salty potato chips are good with rich, cheesy dips; or use simple pitta with spiced dips, etc. If unsure, it's best to stick to plain or salted varieties to avoid any flavour clashes.

Crackers Seeded and whole-grain crackers are good all-rounders but work particularly well with bean and pulse-based dips as their nuttiness complements both the earthy flavour and texture of these wholesome dips.

Crudités Batons and strips of crisp vegetables are a healthy and colourful choice. Choose from raw carrots, celery, sweet (bell) peppers, cucumbers, radishes and chicory/endive leaves to create a classic selection. If you want to add interest, you can also use baby corn, asparagus spears, sugar snap peas, broccoli and cauliflower florets, but these are all best if blanched for just a minute or two before serving.

Bread Soft, fresh bread is good for absorbing light dips. Cubes of focaccia and slices of fresh baguette/French stick work well. Middle-eastern style breads such as pitta and lavash are better sliced into strips and lightly toasted to give them a firmer texture. Ditto for oven-baked crostini toasts, which make excellent crispy dippers. A good tip is to buy part-baked baguettes/French sticks which are easier to slice very thinly. Then simply brush your slices on both sides with olive oil and bake on a tray in an oven preheated to 180°C (350°F) Gas 4 for 8–10 minutes until light brown and crispy. Crostini also have the advantage of keeping in an airtight container for up to 5 days, so can be made in batches in advance and stored.

CHAPTER 1
Classic

Everyday go-to dips

Classic hummus

This hugely popular tasty, nutty-flavoured Middle Eastern dip is so easy to make at home. Serve it with pitta bread, falafel or vegetable crudités as a snack or alongside other mezze dishes for a light meal.

125 g/¾ cup dried chickpeas/
   garbanzo beans

1 teaspoon bicarbonate of soda/
   baking soda

salt

2 garlic cloves, peeled and
   crushed to a paste in a mortar
   with a pestle

4 tablespoons tahini

freshly squeezed juice of 1 lemon

toasted or griddled pitta bread,
   to serve

TO GARNISH

extra virgin olive oil

paprika or sumac

finely chopped fresh flat-leaf
   parsley

SERVES 4–6

Soak the chickpeas overnight in plenty of cold water with the bicarbonate of soda.

Next day, drain and rinse. Put in a large pan, add enough fresh cold water to cover well and bring to the boil. Reduce the heat and simmer for 50–60 minutes until tender, skimming off any scum. Season the chickpeas with salt, then drain, reserving the cooking water and setting aside 1 tablespoon of the cooked chickpeas for the garnish.

In a food processor, blend together the cooked chickpeas, garlic, tahini and lemon juice. Gradually add the cooking liquid until the mixture becomes a smooth paste. Season with salt.

Transfer the hummus to a serving bowl. To serve, make a shallow hollow in the centre using the back of a spoon. Pour in a little olive oil, top with the reserved whole chickpeas, a sprinkle of paprika or sumac and the chopped parsley. Serve with toasted or griddled pitta bread.

Variations

Roast garlic hummus Preheat the oven to 180°C (350°F) Gas 4. Cut about 1-cm/½-in. off the top of a whole bulb of garlic and discard. Loosely wrap the garlic in foil and roast in the preheated oven for about 45 minutes until very soft. Let cool. Squeeze the soft garlic cloves out of their skins and add to the chickpeas when blending.

Griddled vegetable hummus On a barbecue/grill or in a griddle/grill pan, cook slices of sweet red or yellow (bell) pepper, aubergine/eggplant and/or courgette/zucchini that have been tossed with a little olive oil. Add to the chickpeas when you blend them.

Roasted red pepper & chickpea hummus

This delightfully quick and easy hummus is perfect as it comes, but is even better with a bit of tangy feta cheese crumbled over the top.

50 g/2 oz. roasted red (bell) peppers from a jar or can

400-g/14-oz. can chickpeas/ garbanzo beans, drained (reserve a splash of the liquid)

3 tablespoons extra virgin olive oil

1 garlic clove, lightly crushed

2 teaspoons freshly squeezed lemon juice

½ fresh red chilli/chile (optional)

½ teaspoon salt

a little crumbled feta cheese (optional)

MAKES ABOUT 500 G/2 CUPS

Add all the ingredients to a food processor (including a splash of chickpea liquid) and blitz until you have a smooth paste. Taste for seasoning, adding more lemon juice and/or salt as preferred. Transfer to a serving bowl. If you wish, sprinkle a little crumbled feta over the top.

Feel free to add any soft green herbs you like to the food processor as another option (fresh basil works very well with the red pepper).

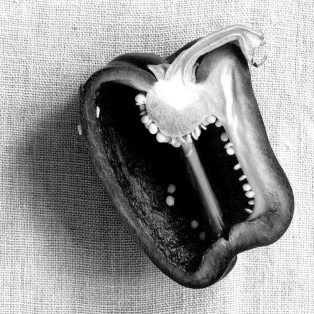

Tomato salsas

Nothing beats a simple, refreshing and appealingly textured relish, to serve alongside cold meat platters, atop hamburgers or as part of a Mexican feast. These four variations use the same tomato base to offer vibrant, colourful, tropical-tasting, summertime salsas that add a zingy taste to any plate.

TOMATO, APPLE & TARRAGON

300 g/10 oz. tomatoes

1 apple, peeled, cored and diced

freshly squeezed juice of ½ lemon

3 teaspoons finely chopped fresh tarragon leaves

salt and freshly ground black pepper

TOMATO & SWEETCORN

300 g/10 oz. tomatoes

the kernels from 1 cob/ear of corn

1 tablespoon finely chopped red onion

2 tablespoons chopped fresh coriander/cilantro

1 tablespoon olive oil

1 teaspoon white wine vinegar

a pinch of smoked paprika

salt and freshly ground black pepper

TOMATO & MANGO

300 g/10 oz. tomatoes

1 ripe mango, peeled, pitted and diced

4 tablespoons chopped fresh coriander/cilantro

grated zest and freshly squeezed juice of ½ lime

1 tablespoon olive oil

salt and freshly ground black pepper

CHILLI TOMATO

300 g/10 oz. tomatoes

2 red chillies/chiles (see method Note)

1 garlic clove, peeled and crushed

2 tablespoons extra virgin olive oil

1 teaspoon balsamic vinegar

2 tablespoons chopped fresh coriander/cilantro

salt and freshly ground black pepper

ALL SERVE 4

For each of the salsas, halve the tomatoes and scoop out the soft seedy pulp, creating tomato shells. Finely dice the tomato shells, discarding the hard, white, stem base.

In a bowl, toss together the diced tomato and all the remaining ingredients for your chosen salsa. Season with salt and black pepper, and serve.

Note: To prepare the chillies, grill/broil them until charred on all sides. Wrap in a plastic bag (so that the steam will make them easier to peel) and set aside to cool. Once cool, peel, deseed and finely chop the chillies, being careful to wash your hands thoroughly after handling. Once prepared, use the chopped chillies following the method above.

Taramasalata

This delicious Greek dip is easier to make from scratch than you might think. Using a decent blender is key, as the texture should be smooth and light. Serve with olives and plenty of toasted pitta bread for a light lunch or snack, or as part of a mezze feast with other dips and small plates.

200 g/7 oz. can cod roe, drained

1 small red onion, grated

½ teaspoon cayenne pepper

2 tablespoons freshly squeezed lemon juice

1 chunky slice of toasted bread

50 ml/3½ tablespoons milk

100 ml/7 tablespoons extra virgin olive oil, plus extra to serve

salt and freshly ground black pepper

TO SERVE

olives

toasted pitta bread

MAKES ABOUT 500 G/2 CUPS

Add the drained cod roe to a food processor, breaking it up with the back of a fork, then add the grated onion, cayenne pepper and lemon juice and season generously with salt and black pepper.

Soak the toasted bread in the milk for a minute, then squeeze out the excess liquid and tear the toast into the food processor (discard the leftover milk). Pulse everything in the food processor to begin with, then increase the speed and start drizzling in the olive oil until it has all been added.

Add a couple of tablespoons of water at the end to smooth the taramasalata if needed. Taste, adding more salt, lemon juice or cayenne as preferred.

Serve in a bowl with a little extra drizzle of olive oil, a few olives alongside and some toasted pitta bread for dipping.

Creamy fava & chicory dip

This soft, creamy mixture of puréed dried broad/fava beans is found in Puglia, southern Italy, where it is called *'ncapriata* or *fave e cicoria*. A similar dish called *'macco'* is served in Sicily, where it is often mixed with wild fennel. The delicious dip itself is made from split dried beans that are already shelled, so you can skip that laborious task.

250 g/1⅓ cups split dried broad/fava beans

1 medium potato, peeled and diced

100 ml/½ cup olive oil, plus extra for frying

500 g/1 lb. chicory/endive

2 garlic cloves, crushed

salt

extra virgin olive oil, to drizzle

toasted sourdough bread, to serve

SERVES 4–6

In a large saucepan, boil the beans and potato in enough water to cover the beans by 4 cm/2 in. for about 1 hour. Add more boiling water during cooking if the mixture gets too dry. By the time the beans are cooked, most of the water should have been absorbed. Beat in the olive oil until you have a thick, smooth purée, then season well with salt.

Meanwhile, boil or steam the chicory. While cooking, heat a tablespoon of olive oil in a frying pan/skillet, and gently sauté the garlic, then toss the drained chicory in the garlicky oil.

To serve, spoon the dip into a bowl and top with the garlicky chicory. Drizzle with some good olive oil and serve with slices of toasted sourdough bread.

Cucumber, mint & dill tzatziki

A Greek classic, this creamy combination of yogurt, cucumber with fresh mint and dill is so simple to make but uniquely refreshing.

1 large, firm cucumber
½ teaspoon salt, plus 2 pinches
400 g/2 scant cups Greek/US strained plain yogurt
2 tablespoons freshly chopped mint and dill, plus extra sprigs to garnish
2 garlic cloves, peeled and crushed
1 tablespoon olive oil

SERVES 4–6

Peel, deseed and dice the cucumber, reserve a little to garnish. Sprinkle the rest of it with ½ teaspoon salt, mix well and set aside for 5 minutes. Wrap the cucumber in a spotlessly clean kitchen towel and squeeze to remove the liquid.

Put in a bowl, reserving a few pieces to garnish, then add the remaining ingredients. Mix together well and serve, garnished with cucumber and dill, if you like.

Variations
Beetroot/beet tzatziki Add 1 medium raw grated beetroot and 2 tablespoons chopped chives to the mixture.

Olive tzatziki Stir 100 g/¾–1 cup finely chopped pitted black or green olives into the cucumber and yogurt mixture.

Red pepper & feta dip

A traditional Greek dip of roasted sweet peppers with tangy feta. Fresh tomato is added here to bring a sweet sharpness, but if you want something a little more sultry, you can use sun-dried tomatoes instead. Like many dips, this one also works really well as a marinade on meat, fish or veggies.

2 red (bell) peppers, halved, pith and seeds removed
4 garlic cloves, unpeeled
4 sprigs of fresh thyme
4 tablespoons olive oil, plus extra for drizzling
a few drops of freshly squeezed lemon juice
a small pinch of cayenne pepper
1 ripe vine tomato (or 2 baby plum tomatoes)
100 g/3½ oz. feta cheese, crumbled
1 tablespoon finely chopped fresh flat-leaf parsley
salt and freshly ground black pepper

SERVES 6

Preheat the oven to 200°C (400°F) Gas 6.

Place the pepper halves onto a baking sheet with a garlic clove and sprig of thyme under each one. Drizzle with olive oil, season with a little salt and pepper and roast in the oven for 20–25 minutes, until they start to char.

Squeeze the roasted garlic cloves out of their skins and drop them into the cup of a blender, followed by the roasted peppers, half the olive oil, the lemon juice, cayenne pepper and tomato. Blend to a pulp. Pour out the mixture, add the crumbled feta, the remaining olive oil and the chopped parsley, and fold through. Serve.

Baba ghanoush

Serve this traditional Middle Eastern-style dip with smoked paprika-dusted pitta chips as a vegetarian appetizer, or with other dishes, such as Classic Hummus (see page 11) or Cucumber, Mint & Dill Tzatziki (see page 19), as part of a bountiful mezze spread.

2 aubergines/eggplants

2 garlic cloves, peeled

1 tablespoon tahini

freshly squeezed juice of ½ lemon

3 tablespoons extra virgin olive oil, plus extra to serve

sea salt

pomegranate seeds, to garnish (optional)

Paprika Pitta Chips (see page 132), to serve

SERVES 4–6

Preheat the oven to 200°C (400°F) Gas 6.

Put the aubergines on a foil-lined baking sheet and roast in the preheated oven for 1 hour, turning over halfway through, until charred on all sides. Put the hot aubergines in a plastic bag (so that the resulting steam will make the skin easier to peel off) and set aside to cool.

Once cool, peel the roasted aubergines and chop the flesh into chunks. Pound the garlic in a mortar with a pestle (with a pinch of salt) until it is a paste.

In a food processor, blend the roast aubergines, garlic paste, lemon juice and olive oil to a smooth purée. Season with salt and cover until ready to serve.

Put the dip in a serving bowl and sprinkle with pomegranate seeds, if using. Drizzle with extra virgin olive oil and serve with the Paprika Pitta Chips on the side for dipping.

Muhammara

This authentic Syrian dip is made from roasted sweet red peppers and earthy walnuts, with a little kick of spice for good measure. Its vibrant colour and tangy flavour provide a wonderful contrast to creamier dips like hummus or tzatziki when served together.

3 large red (bell) peppers

1 slice of day-old sourdough bread, cut into small pieces

100 g/3½ oz. walnut halves, coarsely chopped

½ teaspoon dried red chilli/hot pepper flakes

1 tablespoon sun-dried tomato paste

2 garlic cloves, peeled and chopped

2 teaspoons freshly squeezed lemon juice

1 tablespoon balsamic vinegar

2 teaspoons caster/granulated sugar

1 teaspoon ground cumin

2 tablespoons olive oil

sea salt and freshly ground black pepper

TO SERVE
chopped pistachios
toasted pitta or other flatbread

SERVES 6–8

Cook the peppers one at a time by skewering each one on a fork and holding it directly over a gas flame for 10–15 minutes, until the skin is blackened all over. Alternatively, put them on a baking sheet in an oven preheated to 220°C (425°F) Gas 7. Cook them for about 10–15 minutes, until the skin has puffed up and blackened all over. Transfer to a bowl, cover with clingfilm/plastic wrap and leave until cool enough to handle.

Using your hands, remove the skin and seeds from the peppers and tear the flesh into pieces. Put it in a food processor and add the remaining ingredients. Process to a coarse paste. Season to taste and transfer to a bowl. Cover with clingfilm and refrigerate for 8 hours or ideally overnight before serving.

To serve, bring the dip to room temperature and transfer it to a shallow bowl. Drizzle with olive oil and sprinkle with chopped pistachios. Serve with toasted pitta or flatbread.

Ranch dip

Ranch dip is an all-American classic – perfect for serving at summer parties. It is light and refreshing and bursting with herbs.

60 ml/¼ cup buttermilk

150 g/5½ oz. cream cheese

40 ml/2½ tablespoons mayonnaise

1 garlic clove, peeled and chopped

1 tablespoon olive oil

freshly squeezed juice of ½ lemon

1 tablespoon chopped fresh chives

1 tablespoon chopped fresh
  parsley

1 tablespoon chopped fresh dill

½ teaspoon paprika

1 teaspoon Dijon mustard

salt and freshly ground black
  pepper

Vegetable Crisps/Chips (see page
  131), to serve

SERVES 6–8

In a bowl, whisk together the buttermilk, cream cheese and mayonnaise until smooth.

Put the garlic, olive oil, lemon juice, chives, parsley and dill in a food processor and blitz until very finely chopped and the oil has emulsified. Make sure that there are no large pieces of garlic.

Fold the herb oil into the cream cheese mixture with the paprika and mustard, mixing well so that it is all combined. Season with salt and pepper.

Spoon into a serving bowl and serve with Vegetable Crisps/Chips.

Variation: Cheddar, bacon & onion ranch dip Fry/sauté 4 rashers/slices of lean bacon until crisp and chop into small pieces. Allow to cool and stir into the dip (omitting the dill from the original recipe), along with 4 tablespoons grated Cheddar cheese. Garnish with a handful of chopped spring onions/scallions and serve with giant pretzels for dipping.

French onion dip

When onions are roasted, they develop a sweet caramel flavour, perfect for this dip, which is something of a retro classic. Here it is served with deliciously light and crunchy Homemade Classic Potato Crisps/Chips.

4 medium brown onions

5 sprigs of fresh thyme

2 tablespoons olive oil

250 g/9 oz. cream cheese, at room temperature

3 tablespoons crème fraîche

salt and freshly ground black pepper

Homemade Potato Crisps/Chips (see page 136) or crackers, to serve

SERVES 6

Preheat the oven to 180°C (350°F) Gas 4.

Peel the onions and cut them into quarters. Put the onions in a roasting pan, add the thyme sprigs and drizzle with the olive oil. Season well with salt and pepper and bake in the preheated oven for 30–40 minutes until the onions are soft and have started to caramelize. Give them a stir towards the end of cooking so they don't burn. Remove from the oven and leave to cool. Discard any onions that have gone black as they will add bitterness to the dip.

Remove the thyme sprigs and run your fingers along them to remove the leaves, reserving one sprig for garnish, if you wish. Add the leaves and onions in their cooking juices to a blender and blitz to a smooth purée.

Whisk the cream cheese into the crème fraîche and blend with the onion purée. Taste for seasoning, adding more salt and black pepper if needed.

Spoon the dip into a bowl and garnish with the reserved thyme leaves. Serve with the Homemade Potato Crisps/Chips.

Blue cheese & walnut dip

If you prefer a really strong blue cheese, replace the Gorgonzola Dolce with Stilton or another hard blue cheese and blitz in a blender with the sour cream until smooth before adding to the dip.

100 g/3½ oz. walnut pieces or halves

1 teaspoon finely chopped fresh rosemary

½ teaspoon finely grated lemon zest

1 tablespoon olive oil

1 teaspoon caster/granulated sugar

100 g/½ cup cream cheese

80 g/3 oz. Gorgonzola Dolce or other creamy blue cheese

60 ml/¼ cup sour cream

salt and freshly ground black pepper

celery sticks, green apple wedges or breadsticks, to serve

SERVES 4–6

Preheat the oven to 180°C (350°F) Gas 4.

Put the walnuts, rosemary and lemon zest in a baking pan and drizzle with the olive oil. Sprinkle over the sugar and season with salt and pepper. Shake the pan so that all the nuts are coated in the oil and herbs. Bake in the preheated oven for about 5 minutes until the nuts are hot, taking care that they do not burn. Remove from the oven and leave to cool.

Blitz three-quarters of the walnuts in a food processor or blender. Tip the ground nuts into a bowl with the cream cheese, blue cheese and sour cream and whisk together until smooth and creamy with a slight nutty crunch. Season to taste. Spoon the dip into a bowl and sprinkle over the remaining roasted nuts.

Serve with celery sticks, apple wedges or breadsticks.

Maryland crab dip

A rich and creamy dip with mild, spicy heat. For a twist, fold in chopped lobster or shrimp in place of the crab.

150 g/5½ oz. cream cheese

125 ml/½ cup buttermilk

2 tablespoons mayonnaise

1 tablespoon hot chilli sauce (such as Frank's)

freshly ground black pepper

freshly squeezed juice of 1 lemon

120 g/4½ oz. Cheddar cheese or provolone, grated

100 g/3½ oz. white or brown crabmeat

a pinch of chilli/chili powder

3 tablespoons panko breadcrumbs

celery sticks, to serve

SERVES 6–8

Preheat the oven to 180°C (350°F) Gas 4.

Place the cream cheese, buttermilk and mayonnaise in a bowl and whisk together until smooth. Add the hot sauce, a grind of black pepper and the lemon juice, and whisk to combine.

Divide the grated cheese into ⅔ and ⅓. Add the larger portion of cheese to the cream cheese mixture along with the crabmeat and chilli/chili powder, and fold together gently until mixed. Spoon into an ovenproof bowl. Cover the top with the remaining cheese and sprinkle over the panko breadcrumbs.

Bake in the preheated oven for 20–25 minutes until the cheese on top is golden brown. Remove from the oven and leave to cool for 10 minutes before serving with celery sticks for dipping.

Mont d'Or dip

Mont d'Or, or Vacherin Mont d'Or, is a cow's milk cheese from Switzerland, named after the mountain itself. Wrapped traditionally in a spruce box to help contain the flavours within, it is one of the world's most celebrated cheeses. Part of the reason for this is it is only produced in winter, meaning availability is limited. Eaten *au naturel*, you cut away the top rind and scoop out the unctuous centre. Baked whole in its box, the cheese melts to a gooey, almost liquid perfection and is best served with breadsticks or potato crisps/chips.

1 small Mont d'Or cheese, 490 g/
    1 lb. 2 oz., at room temperature

2 garlic cloves, thinly sliced

2 sprigs of fresh rosemary, leaves
    picked

60 ml/4 tablespoons Jura wine
    or dry fino sherry

a drizzle of extra virgin olive oil

coarsely ground black pepper

Grissini (see page 134) and/or
    purple potato crisps/chips,
    to serve

SERVES 4–6

Preheat the oven to 200°C (400°F) Gas 6 and line a baking pan with baking paper.

Discard the wooden lid from the Mont d'Or box. Make lots of small cuts in the top of the cheese and carefully poke in the garlic slices and rosemary leaves. Pour the wine and olive oil over the cheese and season with pepper.

Place in the prepared pan and bake for 25–30 minutes or until the cheese is molten, bubbling and lightly golden.

Stir the melted cheese mixture until smooth, then transfer to a platter and serve with Grissini or potato crisps/chips for dipping.

CHAPTER 2

Virtuous

Lighter, healthier dips

Spinach hummus

This vibrant dip is a great way to get more greens into your diet. It's important not to over-cook green leafy vegetables to avoid losing nutrients. They can also be used raw, like here in the following recipe; this way, all the nutrients remain and the hummus becomes a beautiful green!

320 g/2 cups cooked chickpeas/ garbanzo beans, plus 60 ml/ ¼ cup of the cooking liquid, or more if needed

3 tablespoons extra virgin olive oil

1 tablespoon cashew butter

3 garlic cloves

1 tablespoon umeboshi vinegar (optional)

70 g/1 handful raw spinach leaves

freshly squeezed juice of ½ lemon, or to taste

½ teaspoon salt, or to taste

freshly chopped flat-leaf parsley, to garnish (optional)

Vegetable Crisps/Chips (see page 131), to serve (optional)

SERVES 2–3

Blend all the ingredients in a blender or food processor, slowly adding the cooking liquid until you reach a thick and creamy consistency; this will take about 1 minute. (High-speed blenders make the creamiest texture and need less liquid and time, but both food processors and stick blenders can be used as well.)

Adjust the lemon juice and salt to taste. Garnish with chopped flat-leaf parsley, if you like, and serve with Vegetable Crisps/Chips for dipping.

Flax-speckled hummus
with kale crisps/chips

It's so easy to make your own hummus. This recipe is a double dose of flax because it uses both flaxseeds and flaxseed oil, so it's a great source of omega 3s. Kale, one of the best green superfoods, is delicious as a crisp/chip for dipping.

400 g/3 cups cooked chickpeas/
  garbanzo beans

2 tablespoons tahini paste

freshly squeezed juice of 2 large
  lemons

2 tablespoons water

2 garlic cloves, crushed

1 teaspoon ground cumin

1 tablespoon flaxseed oil

1 tablespoon milled flaxseeds

sea salt and freshly ground black
  pepper, to taste

KALE CRISPS/CHIPS

1 medium head of curly kale

2 tablespoons olive oil

1 tablespoon Parmesan cheese
  or nutritional yeast flakes if you
  are dairy-free

1 teaspoon onion powder or
  2 small chopped onions

½ teaspoon Himalayan salt

SERVES 4

For the hummus, simply blend all of the ingredients in a food processor until smooth.

For the kale crisps/chips, preheat the oven to 95ºC (200ºF) Gas ¼.

Wash and dry the kale. Mix the oil, Parmesan or nutritional yeast flakes, onion powder or chopped onion and salt in a bowl. Add the kale leaves to the bowl and coat with the oil mixture. Put the kale leaves on a baking sheet and cook in the preheated oven for 45 minutes. Keep an eye on them so as not to burn the edges.

Cool and serve with the hummus or store in an airtight container for up to 3 days.

Broad bean & ricotta dip

A fresh-tasting dip, with a pleasant nutty taste. Serve with strips of warm toasted pitta bread or vegetable crudités.

250 g/9 oz. fresh or frozen broad/fava beans

2 garlic cloves, crushed

1 tablespoon olive oil

100 g/½ cup ricotta cheese

2 tablespoons chopped fresh dill, plus extra to garnish

salt and freshly ground black pepper

toasted pitta bread or crudités, to serve

SERVES 4

Preheat the oven to 180°C (350°F) Gas 4.

Cook the beans in a saucepan of boiling water until just tender. Drain, cool and pop the beans out of their skins.

Put the skinned beans, garlic and olive oil in a food processor and blend together; alternatively mash together in a bowl using a fork. Add the ricotta, chopped dill, salt and pepper and mix briefly.

Spoon the dip into a bowl, garnish with dill fronds and serve with warm toasted pitta bread or vegetable crudités.

Roast carrot, ginger & miso dip

Roasted carrots make a deliciously creamy and sweet dip. The ginger adds a welcome spicy heat and the miso (fermented soya bean paste) brings a deliciously savoury note.

300 g/10½ oz. carrots, peeled and thinly sliced

25 g/1 oz. grated fresh ginger

3 tablespoons white miso paste

2 tablespoons tahini

black and white sesame seeds, to garnish (optional)

tortilla chips or crackers, to serve

SERVES 4

Preheat the oven to 180°C (350°F) Gas 4.

Put the carrots in a roasting pan and roast in the preheated oven for about 20–25 minutes until softened but not browned. Set aside until cool.

Blitz the cooled carrots in a food processor or blender together with the ginger, miso and tahini. Spoon into a bowl, garnish with a sprinkling of sesame seeds, if using, and serve with tortilla chips or crackers.

Edamame & wasabi dip

Edamame (soy) beans are a rare plant source of Omega-3 fatty acids, so this delicious green dip packs a nutritional punch as well as making a lighter alternative to hummus.

200 g/1½ cups shelled edamame beans (fresh, or frozen and thawed)

3 tablespoons sweet white miso paste

1 tablespoon extra virgin olive oil

1 tablespoon tamari soy sauce

1 teaspoon wasabi paste

vegetable crudités or breadsticks, to serve

SERVES 2–3

Put most of the edamame beans (reserving some to garnish) and 1 tablespoon water in a food processor and blitz until smooth. Add the remaining ingredients and mix well so that everything is well incorporated.

Spoon into a bowl, top with the reserved edamame beans and serve with crudités or breadsticks.

Pea, feta & fresh mint dip

This dip is ideal for serving at an al fresco summer lunch. It is light and creamy with a perfect saltiness from the feta, and hints of lemon and mint make it really refreshing.

250g/9 oz. frozen peas
3 sprigs of fresh mint
grated zest and juice of 1 lemon
200g/7 oz. feta cheese
150g/5½ oz. cream cheese
salt and freshly ground black
   pepper

TO SERVE
peashoots, to garnish (optional)
olive oil
Paprika Pitta Chips (see page 132)
   or Bagel Toasts (see page 133)

SERVES 4

Bring a saucepan of water to the boil and simmer the peas with the mint and a pinch of salt for about 5 minutes until cooked. Drain and blanch in cold water until the peas are cold.

Drain the peas and add to a blender with the mint and the lemon juice. Blitz to a purée but keep some texture to it. If you prefer a very smooth dip you can pass the pea mixture through a fine mesh sieve/strainer using a rubber spatula or spoon.

Crumble the feta into a mixing bowl, then whisk together with the cream cheese until smooth. Add the lemon zest, pea purée and a good grinding of black pepper and whisk again.

Spoon into a bowl and garnish with peashoots, if using, and a drizzle of olive oil. Serve with Paprika Pitta Crisps/Chips or Bagel Toasts for dipping.

Beetroot herb dip with seeded amaranth crackers

You eat with your eyes first with this dip... Beetroot/beet is as nutritious as it is colourful. Sumac is a versatile North African and Middle Eastern spice, also used in the spice blend Za'atar. You can make the crackers purely from seeds, which would be nutty and delicious, but it's nice to add a bit of amaranth flour to give them a little more substance while still retaining a crispy texture.

2 garlic bulbs, unpeeled

4 beetroot/beets, tops and bottoms trimmed

3 tablespoons flaxseed oil

1½ teaspoons ground sumac

1 teaspoon cumin seeds

freshly squeezed juice of 1 lemon

1 teaspoon sea salt

freshly ground black pepper, to taste

a handful of fresh coriander/ cilantro, to garnish

AMARANTH CRACKERS

45 g/⅓ cup amaranth flour

40 g/⅓ cup milled flaxseeds

40 g/¼ cup sunflower seeds

1 teaspoon sea salt

¼ teaspoon onion powder or ½ small chopped onion

20 g/⅛ cup pumpkin seeds

2 tablespoons milled hemp seeds

1 tablespoon melted coconut oil, plus extra for greasing

60 ml/¼ cup water

SERVES 4

For the dip, preheat the oven to 180°C (350°F) Gas 4.

Wrap the garlic in foil and put on one of the prepared baking sheets. Wrap the beetroot in a separate sheet of foil and put on the same baking sheet. Roast the beetroot and garlic for about 30 minutes in the preheated oven, then remove the garlic and set aside. Roast the beetroot for a further 30 minutes or until tender, then allow to cool.

Peel the garlic and the beetroot (this is the messy part so feel free to wear gloves!) and blend them in a food processor with the flaxseed oil, sumac, cumin seeds, lemon juice, salt and pepper. Add more flaxseed oil as needed to reach the desired consistency.

For the crackers, preheat the oven to 150°C (300°F) Gas 2. Grease the second prepared baking sheet with a thin layer of coconut oil.

Pulse all of the dry ingredients in a food processor – you can leave the seeds in a roughly chopped state, if you prefer more texture. Then add the coconut oil and water and blend again until all the ingredients come together into a dough. Roll the dough thinly onto the prepared baking sheet and bake in the preheated oven for 45–50 minutes. Set aside to cool, then break into pieces. Store in an airtight container until ready to serve.

Transfer the dip to a serving bowl, garnish with fresh coriander and serve with the crackers.

Butter bean whip & crudités platter

Perfect for your vegan and vegetarian guests and all lovers of vegetables. The butter/lima bean whip, with its citrus and garlic mix, is topped with sautéed spring onions/scallions, herbs and capers and is a taste sensation. Arrange your vegetables and crackers in groups with edible flowers for added decoration if you wish.

400-g/14-oz. can butter/lima beans, drained

2 tablespoons olive oil

1 teaspoon sea salt, or to taste

1 garlic clove, crushed

freshly squeezed juice of 1 lemon

freshly ground black pepper

vegetable crudités and/or crackers, to serve

TOPPING

2 tablespoons olive oil

2 sprigs of fresh rosemary, leaves picked

8 fresh sage leaves

2 sprigs of fresh tarragon, leaves picked

2 spring onions/scallions, finely sliced

2 teaspoons capers, drained

grated zest of 1 lemon

SERVES 4

For the dip, using a food processor or hand-held electric/stick blender, blend the beans, oil, ½ teaspoon salt, garlic, lemon juice and pepper. Taste and add the remaining salt if necessary.

For the topping, heat the oil in a sauté pan over a medium heat. Carefully add the herbs, spring onions and capers to the hot oil and fry for 1–2 minutes until crisp. Use a slotted spoon to carefully transfer the fried topping to paper towels to drain off any excess oil, reserving the oil in the pan.

To assemble, use a spatula or the back of a spoon to spread the bean dip over a nice plate or bowl. Top with the crispy herbs and a few splashes of the infused pan oil. Sprinkle over the lemon zest and serve with crudités and/or crackers.

Zesty almond & herb pesto

Traditionally pesto is made with basil, pine nuts and Parmesan, but this cheese-free version is made with a mixture of fresh green herbs and almonds. The zesty taste comes from the lemon zest and kaffir lime leaf. If you can't find kaffir lime, feel free to use lemongrass instead.

20 g/¾ oz. fresh baby spinach leaves
leaves from 1 small bunch each fresh mint, flat-leaf parsley and coriander/cilantro
30 g/¼ cup blanched almonds
6 tablespoons extra virgin olive oil, plus extra to preserve
1 kaffir lime leaf
freshly squeezed juice of 1 lime
grated zest of 1 lemon
1 garlic clove, peeled
a pinch of sea salt
vegetable crudités or breadsticks, to serve

SERVES 2

Put all the ingredients in a food processor and blitz until they form a paste.

Spoon into a dish and serve immediately with crudités, such as carrots and cucumber batons, or breadsticks, for dipping. (Be aware that the herbs will oxidize and the dip will loose its vibrant green colour fairly quickly after making so it's important to serve it very fresh.)

Lighter guacamole

Although traditional guacamole is made with fresh healthy ingredients, it does have a high calorie content. This version has been lightened up with the inclusion of fresh peas and (bell) peppers. It keeps its creamy texture and body, but makes it a lighter option.

1 large avocado, peeled and pitted
90 g/3 oz. peas (ideally fresh, but frozen and thawed is fine too)
½ red (bell) pepper, deseeded
2 tomatoes
¼ small onion
1 garlic clove, peeled
large handful of fresh coriander/cilantro
freshly squeezed juice of ½ lime
1 tablespoon freshly squeezed lemon juice, plus extra to preserve
vegetable crudités or breadsticks, to serve

SERVES 2

Put all the ingredients in a food processor and blitz until smooth.

Spoon into a dish and serve immediately with crudités, such as carrot batons, or breadsticks, for dipping. (Be aware that the avocado will quickly brown and the dip will loose its vibrant green colour fairly quickly after making so it's important to serve it very fresh.)

White bean & spinach dip

This is a beautifully, light and nutritious green dip that looks great garnished with fresh herbs and served with crunchy crostini.

410 g/2½ cups cooked white
  beans, drained
freshly squeezed juice of 1 lemon
freshly squeezed juice of 1 small
  orange
1 garlic clove, peeled
3 tablespoons flaxseed oil
50 g/2 oz. fresh spinach leaves
salt and freshly ground black
  pepper
Crostini (see page 137), to serve

SERVES 4–6

Blend all of the dip ingredients, except the spinach, together in a food processor until blended but still chunky in texture.

Coarsely chop the spinach and stir into the dip mixture. Season to taste with salt and freshly ground black pepper.

Spoon the dip into a bowl and serve with the Crostini on the side.

Pea & basil hummus

This thick, hummus-like dip made with green peas is a great one for a summer lunch spread. It has an amazing smooth texture, strong flavour and punchy colour. A simple recipe, but-oh so delicious.

720 ml/3 cups water

260 g/2 cups fresh or frozen peas

10 g/½ cup fresh basil, plus a few leaves to garnish

1 tablespoon olive oil, plus extra for drizzling

2 garlic cloves

2 tablespoons sunflower seed butter

½ teaspoon cumin seeds, dry-roasted and crushed (optional)

½ teaspoon salt, or to taste

SERVES 2–4

Bring a pan of water to the boil, add the peas and cook, covered, until soft but still green (about 8–10 minutes). Drain, saving the cooking water.

Blend the peas in a food processor or blender with all the other ingredients until thick and creamy, adding about 60 ml/¼ cup of the cooking liquid as necessary. Drizzle with extra olive oil to serve, if you like.

Artichoke tarator

Tarator is a tasty Turkish garlic and nut dip, and this version has artichokes to make it extra special. Perfect as a dip with vegetable crudités – it goes especially well with the bitterness of chicory/endive.

2 slices of day-old bread, crusts removed
6 canned artichoke hearts, drained
freshly squeezed juice of 1 lemon
3–4 garlic cloves, peeled and crushed
½ teaspoon salt
70 g/2½ oz. blanched almonds, finely chopped
4 tablespoons olive oil, plus extra to serve
toasted flaked/slivered almonds, to garnish
endive/chicory or bread cubes, to serve

SERVES 2–3

Put the bread in a sieve/strainer and pour over boiling water; when cool enough to handle, squeeze out any excess water.

Chop the artichoke hearts and put in a food processor with the bread, lemon juice, garlic, salt and almonds. Blend together, adding the oil slowly to combine.

Spoon into a bowl, drizzle with extra oil and scatter with the flaked almonds. Serve with endive leaves for scooping, or cubes of bread, as preferred.

Zhug

Fiery and versatile, zhug ('zhoug') is a popular chilli/chile paste from Yemen that can be used as a dip, marinade or condiment. Packed full of punchy ingredients, a little goes a long way.

8 dried red chillies/chiles (Horn or New Mexico varieties)
4 garlic cloves, roughly chopped
1 teaspoon salt
seeds of 4–6 cardamom pods
1 teaspoon caraway seeds
½ teaspoon black peppercorns
a small bunch fresh flat-leaf parsley, finely chopped
a small bunch of fresh coriander/cilantro, finely chopped
3–4 tablespoons olive oil or sunflower oil

large sterilized glass jar

SERVES 2–3

Put the chillies in a bowl, pour boiling water over them and leave them to soak for at least 6 hours. Drain them, cut off the stalks, squeeze out the seeds, and roughly chop them.

Using a pestle and mortar, pound the chillies with the garlic and salt to a thick, smooth paste. Add the cardamom and caraway seeds and the peppercorns and pound them with the chilli paste – you want to break up the seeds and peppercorns, but they don't have to be perfectly ground as a little bit of texture is good. Beat in the parsley and coriander and bind the mixture with the oil.

Spoon the spice paste into a sterilized jar, drizzle the rest of the oil over the top and keep it in a cool place, or in the refrigerator, for up to 4 weeks. When serving as a condiment or a dip for bread, mix the layer of oil into it and garnish with finely chopped coriander or parsley.

CHAPTER 3
Wholesome

Hearty & nourishing dips

Black bean dip
with blue corn chips

Black beans are very popular in Mexican cookery, and here they are used to make a spicy dip, which has a fresh taste of lime, coriander/cilantro and tomato. Serve with freshly made blue corn chips.

230 g/½ lb. cooked black beans, drained weight

2 spring onions/scallions, trimmed

freshly squeezed juice of 2 limes

15 g/½ oz. fresh coriander/cilantro, plus extra to serve

100 g/3½ oz. block of creamed coconut

1–2 red chillies/chiles, depending on heat required, deseeded

1 teaspoon soft dark brown sugar

2–3 tablespoons plain yogurt

10 cherry tomatoes

salt and freshly ground black pepper

olive oil, to drizzle

BLUE CORN CHIPS
8 soft blue corn tortillas

salt

SERVES 6–8

Drain the black beans in a sieve/strainer and rinse under cold water. Reserve a spoonful of the beans for garnish, then put the rest in a food processor or blender with the spring onions, lime juice, coriander, creamed coconut, chillies and sugar and blitz until smooth. Season with salt and pepper to taste. Add 2–3 spoonfuls of yogurt to loosen the dip as required.

Deseed the tomatoes and chop into small pieces. Reserve a spoonful of the chopped tomatoes for garnish, then fold the rest into the dip.

To make the blue corn chips, preheat the oven to 200°C (400°F) Gas 6. Stack the tortillas and, using a sharp knife or scissors, cut them into even-sized triangles – you choose the size you want!

Spread them out in a single layer over 2 baking sheets, spacing them at least 5-mm/¼-in. apart. Shake salt over them. Bake in the preheated oven for 8–12 minutes until starting to get crispy and slightly golden brown at the edges.

Spoon the dip into a serving bowl and top with the reserved tomato and beans and garnish with extra fresh coriander. Drizzle with a little olive oil and serve with the blue corn chips.

Sweet potato hummus

This velvety-smooth sweet potato hummus dip makes an interesting change from the more familiar chickpea-only version. The herby breadsticks are surprisingly simple to make and their crunchy texture makes them the perfect accompaniment here.

1 sweet potato, unpeeled

3 garlic cloves, unpeeled

½ x 400-g/14-oz. can of chickpeas/garbanzo beans

1 fresh red chilli/chile, finely chopped

a handful of fresh coriander/cilantro leaves, chopped

2 tablespoons olive oil

grated zest and freshly squeezed juice of ½ lime

salt and freshly ground black pepper

Herby Breadsticks (see page 133), to serve

SERVES 4–6

Preheat the oven to 180°C (350°F) Gas 4.

Roast the sweet potato in a roasting pan in the preheated oven for 30–40 minutes until very soft. Add the garlic cloves to the pan about 20 minutes before the end of the cooking time. Remove from the oven and, when cool enough to handle, remove and discard the skins from the sweet potato and garlic cloves.

Put in a food processor along with the chickpeas, chilli, coriander, olive oil and lime zest and blitz until it reaches the desired consistency. Season with salt, pepper and lime juice to taste.

When ready to serve, spoon the sweet potato hummus into a serving bowl and serve with the Herby Breadsticks.

Macadamia & chilli dip

This is a variation on a peanut satay dip. It's particularly good with Vegetable Crisps/Chips (see page 131), or it can be served with crudités.

1 tablespoon macadamia or groundnut oil

1 teaspoon blachan (Thai shrimp paste)

2 garlic cloves, peeled and crushed

4 shallots, finely chopped

125 ml/½ cup coconut cream

1 tablespoon brown sugar

70 g/2½ oz. cup macadamia nuts, toasted

3 large fresh red chillies/chiles, chopped

1 teaspoon finely chopped lemongrass

1 tablespoon soy sauce

Vegetable Crisps/Chips (see page 31), or crudités, to serve

SERVES 2–3

Heat the oil in a small saucepan. Add the blachan and gently fry for 1 minute, breaking it up with a wooden spoon. Add the garlic and shallots and sauté for 3 minutes. Add the coconut cream and sugar and bring to the boil, then reduce to a simmer for 1 minute before removing from the heat.

Put the macadamia nuts, chillies, lemongrass and soy sauce in a blender or small food processor and blend in bursts, adding the coconut cream mixture, a little at a time, until well combined.

Spoon the dip into a dish and serve with Vegetable Crisps/Chips or crudités, as preferred.

Wild garlic & chilli pesto

Homemade pesto pasta is the ultimate quick, delicious supper for all the family. This grown-up variation on a classic pesto sauce introduces a lovely kick of chilli heat and the delicious punch of wild garlic leaves. It works so well as a dip, but leftovers can of course be used to coat pasta too.

75 g/½ cup pine nuts

1 garlic clove, peeled

2 handfuls of wild garlic leaves or fresh purple basil leaves

100 g/1 cup grated Parmesan

4 tablespoons extra virgin olive oil

1 hot green chilli/chile

sea salt and freshly ground black pepper

cubes of foccacia, to serve

SERVES 4

Heat a heavy-based frying pan/skillet over a medium heat, add the pine nuts and dry fry until they begin to brown. Keep them moving so that they toast evenly. Remove from the pan and set aside to cool a little.

Grind 1 teaspoon salt and the garlic to a paste with a pestle and mortar. Put the paste into a food processor with the pine nuts and remaining ingredients. Pulse until you have a smooth paste. Taste and season with a little more salt and some pepper if required. Add more oil if the paste needs to be looser. Serve with cubes of foccacia for dipping.

Walnut & red pepper hummus

This is the ideal choice for all who wish to enjoy the velvety texture of hummus with an extra kick of nutrients provided by raw, fresh ingredients. This hummus can be made well in advance – it will taste even better if it sits in the fridge for a couple of days.

300 g/2 cups walnuts, shelled
80 g/⅔ cup diced onion
½ bunch fresh parsley
2 tablespoons olive oil
1 tablespoon tahini
1 teaspoon salt
¼ teaspoon chilli/chili powder
2 garlic cloves
1 tablespoon sweet paprika
1 red (bell) pepper, seeded
umeboshi vinegar, to taste
   (or substitute with lemon
   juice and a little soy sauce)
mini toasts or crackers, to serve
garlic chives and mixed micro
   cress or herbs, to garnish
   (optional)

SERVES 2–3

Cover the walnuts with plenty of water and let soak for a couple of hours or overnight with a pinch of salt. Rinse and drain.

Blend all the ingredients in a high-speed blender for 1 minute into a velvety hummus. For weaker blenders, you might need to add a little water during blending.

Serve the hummus spread on mini toasts or crackers. Garnish with mixed micro cress and herbs, if you like.

Mediterranean tomato hummus

This hummus is packed full of Mediterranean ingredients. A whole head of garlic is roasted to make the cloves soft, mellow and caramelized, while sun-dried tomatoes and plenty of fresh herbs finish off this aromatic dip.

1 garlic bulb

10 sun-dried tomato halves

320 g/2 cups cooked chickpeas/
  garbanzo beans, plus 60 ml/
  ¼ cup of the cooking liquid,
  or more if needed

1 tablespoon tahini

3 tablespoons extra virgin olive
  oil (2 for the hummus and
  1 to serve)

1 bunch of fresh basil, chopped,
  plus a few whole leaves to
  garnish

1 sprig of fresh thyme, leaves only

3 tablespoons chopped fresh
  parsley leaves

2 teaspoons lemon juice

½ teaspoon salt, or to taste

¼ teaspoon dried rosemary

freshly ground black pepper

coarse sea salt and 1 teaspoon
  olive oil, for baking the garlic

SERVES 2–3

Preheat the oven to 180°C (350°F) Gas 4.

Brush the garlic head with oil, rub in some coarse sea salt, wrap in aluminium foil and bake in the preheated oven for 40 minutes or until the garlic flesh becomes soft. Use half of the amount in this recipe and save the remaining paste to add to other dishes.

Soak the sun-dried tomato halves in warm water for 30 minutes. Drain and discard the soaking water. (If using oil-packed tomato halves, there's no need to soak them, but omit 2 tablespoons of olive oil in the recipe, since the tomatoes will bring enough oil to the hummus.) Chop finely.

Blend the chickpeas with the tahini, slowly adding the cooking liquid, until it has reached the desired consistency.

Spoon the hummus out into a bigger bowl and stir in the chopped tomato halves, half the garlic bulb paste, chopped basil, the thyme leaves, 2 tablespoons of the olive oil, 2 tablespoons of the chopped parsley, the lemon juice, salt and freshly ground black pepper to taste. Sprinkle with the dried rosemary and the remaining chopped parsley, and garnish with the whole basil leaves and a drizzle of olive oil before serving.

Scorched aubergine & cauliflower dip
with onion & pomegranate salad

This is one of those moreish combinations you'll dream about for days.
The dip is smoky, creamy and delicious with the sweet and tart onions.

2 large aubergines/eggplants
(about 650 g/1 lb. 7 oz.)

½ cauliflower, cut into florets
(about 200 g/7 oz.)

4 garlic cloves, unpeeled

1 teaspoon smoked cumin

4 tablespoons extra virgin olive oil

freshly squeezed juice of 1 lemon

2 tablespoons tahini

1 tablespoon each freshly chopped
mint and flat-leaf parsley

1 tablespoon pomegranate seeds

½ teaspoon sumac

salt and freshly ground black
pepper

purple basil, to garnish (optional)

salad
3 red onions

2 tablespoons vegetable oil

4 tablespoons pomegranate
molasses

1 teaspoon maple syrup (optional)

2 teaspoons sumac

1 teaspoon sea salt flakes

*2 wooden skewers, soaked
for 30 minutes*

SERVES 4

Preheat the oven to 200°C (400°F) Gas 6.

Blacken the aubergines over a gas hob/ring or barbecue/outdoor grill, turning regularly with tongs, until completely charred and collapsed. Allow to cool.

Place the cauliflower and garlic on the lined baking sheet and sprinkle with the cumin. Drizzle with 2 tablespoons of the olive oil and season. Bake in the preheated oven for 10 minutes, then turn and cook for another 10 minutes or until tender and the cauliflower has coloured. Squeeze the garlic out of the skins and set aside with the cauliflower to cool.

Slit the aubergines lengthways and scoop out the flesh, discarding the skins. Leave in a sieve/strainer to drain for 30 minutes.

In a serving bowl, stir the lemon juice and 3 tablespoons water into the tahini until it loosens. Add the mint and flat-leaf parsley and season. Mash the aubergines, garlic and cauliflower with a fork (reserving a few cauli florets for garnish), then stir them into the tahini mixture. Top with the reserved florets, pomegranate seeds, sumac and purple basil, if liked. Pour the remaining oil around the edge.

For the salad, peel and quarter the onions, leaving the roots and tips on. Toss the onions in the oil and skewer them. Fry in a very hot griddle/grill pan until charred. Drizzle the hot onions with the molasses and maple syrup, (if using), sprinkle with the sumac and salt flakes. Serve.

Creamy artichoke & spinach dip

This delicious dip can be prepared in a matter of minutes. Using a garlic and herb soft cheese adds instant depth, but if preferred you can substitute with a plain cream cheese and add any finely chopped fresh green herb – basil works well.

80 g/3 oz. fresh baby spinach leaves, washed and stalks removed

1 x 280-g/10-oz. jar chargrilled artichoke hearts in oil (170 g/ 6 oz. drained weight)

20 g/¾ oz. garlic and herb soft cheese (such as Boursin)

40 g/1½ oz. Parmesan cheese, grated

80 g/3 oz. sour cream or crème fraîche

salt and freshly ground black pepper

crostini or thinly sliced toasted sourdough bread, to serve

SERVES 4

Blitz the spinach in a food processor or blender.

Drain the artichoke hearts, roughly chop and add to the food processor or blender with all the remaining ingredients. Blitz until smooth, then season with salt and freshly ground black pepper.

Serve the dip slightly chilled with crostini or toasted sourdough, as preferred.

Broad bean 'guacamole'

There is not an avocado to be found in this recipe, but the blended beans are instantly reminiscent of smashed avocado. It's unapologetically inauthentic, so if you're experiencing an avocado shortage or you're not a big fan of the trendy fruit, try this dip recipe instead. It's also good slathered on toast, topped with a poached egg and a drizzle of hot sauce.

400-g/14-oz. can broad/fava beans (green), drained

½ garlic clove, crushed

60 ml/¼ cup extra virgin olive oil

½ teaspoon salt

1 teaspoon freshly squeezed lime juice

½ teaspoon malt vinegar

a pinch of ground cumin

1 spring onion/scallion, finely sliced

a few sprigs of fresh coriander/cilantro, chopped

SERVES 4

Add all the ingredients, except the spring onion and coriander, to a food processor. Pulse at first, then increase the speed until you have a coarsely puréed consistency.

Fold in the spring onion and coriander and taste, adding more salt, lime juice or cumin as preferred. Transfer to a serving bowl and serve.

Light aubergine dip with almond chia crackers

This recipe is similar to the well known Levantine dip, baba ghanoush, which traditionally contains tahini paste. Here, the tahini has been left out to let the pure flavour of the roasted aubergine take centre stage. It goes beautifully well with the nutty almond chia crackers.

800 g/2 large aubergines/eggplants

2 tablespoons grapeseed oil

½ teaspoon Himalayan salt

2 garlic cloves

2 tablespoons freshly squeezed lemon juice

3 tablespoons flaxseed oil

salt and freshly ground black pepper, to taste

ALMOND CHIA CRACKERS

60 g/½ cup almond flour

30 g/¼ cup coconut flour

30 g/¼ cup ground chia seeds

¾ teaspoon salt

½ teaspoon onion powder or 1 chopped small onion

60 ml/¼ cup olive oil

60 ml/¼ cup water

SERVES 2 (MAKES 12 CRACKERS)

Preheat the oven to 200°C (400°F) Gas 6.

Cut the aubergine in half and pierce the skin and flesh several times. Put on a baking sheet, drizzle with grapeseed oil, sprinkle with salt and bake skin side up in the oven for 35–40 minutes, or until the flesh is tender. Remove from the oven and cool in a bowl of iced water. This will make it easier to peel away the skins.

Peel and discard the skins and add the flesh to the garlic, lemon juice and flaxseed oil in a food processor. Blend, season with salt and pepper and refrigerate until you are ready to serve.

For the crackers, preheat the oven to 180°C (350°F) Gas 4.

Add all of the dry ingredients to a mixing bowl. Add the oil and water and mix to form a ball with your hands. Chill in the refrigerator in clingfilm/plastic wrap for 20 minutes. Roll out the dough as thinly as possible on a non-stick baking sheet.

Bake in the preheated oven for 15 minutes, then remove from the oven, leave to cool and cut into pieces.

Transfer the dip to a serving bowl and serve with the crackers.

Romesco dip with grilled spring onions

Romesco is a Spanish dip made with sweet peppers, almonds, bread and garlic that is traditionally eaten with the first onions/scallions of spring.

6 medium tomatoes, halved

4 red (bell) peppers, halved and deseeded

8 tablespoons olive oil

50 g/generous ⅓ cup hazelnuts or almonds, blanched

15-cm/6-in. piece of stale white baguette/French bread, broken into chunks

3 garlic cloves, peeled

1 tablespoon sherry vinegar

½ teaspoon smoked paprika

12 spring onions/scallions, tops and bottoms trimmed

salt and freshly ground black pepper

SERVES 4–6

Preheat the oven to 200°C (400°F) Gas 6.

Put the tomatoes and peppers in separate roasting pans, season and drizzle 1 tablespoon of the olive oil over each. Roast in the preheated oven for about 35 minutes, or until the pepper skins have started to blacken. Meanwhile, blitz the blanched nuts in a food processor or blender and leave them in there.

Remove the tomatoes from the pan and set aside. Add the chunks of baguette to the tomato juices in the pan. Let cool.

Remove the peppers from the pan, put into a bowl, cover with clingfilm/plastic wrap and allow to cool. Once cooled, remove and discard the pepper skins and add the flesh to the food processor, along with the tomatoes. Add 4 tablespoons of the olive oil, along with the garlic, soaked bread, sherry vinegar and smoked paprika. Blitz until smooth.

To prepare the spring onions/scallions, preheat the grill/broiler to high. Drizzle the remaining olive oil over them and toss to coat. Arrange them on the grill pan and cook, turning, for 3–5 minutes. Serve warm with the romesco dip.

Peanut satay dip

Peanut satay makes a great dip to serve as a snack before a Thai meal with prawn/shrimp crackers and carrot batons to dip. This recipe uses solid creamed coconut, but you can substitute it for a small can of creamed coconut if you need to, though as it's runnier you may not need to add the crème fraîche.

1 tablespoon soy or tamari sauce

1 tablespoon soft dark brown sugar

100-g/3½-oz. block creamed coconut

2 tablespoons crunchy peanut butter

150 g/5½ oz. cream cheese

freshly squeezed juice of 1 lime

2 tablespoons crème fraîche or sour cream

1 tablespoon roasted peanuts, finely chopped, to garnish

fresh coriander/cilantro leaves, to garnish

prawn/shrimp crackers or carrot batons, to serve

SERVES 4–6

In a bowl, whisk the soy sauce and brown sugar together until the sugar has dissolved. Put the mixture in a blender with the creamed coconut, peanut butter, cream cheese and lime juice and blitz until smooth. Fold through the crème fraîche to loosen.

Spoon into a bowl and garnish with chopped peanuts and coriander leaves, if you like. Serve straight away with prawn crackers and carrot batons, for dipping. (Note that if you chill the dip in the refrigerator it will set, so you will need to bring it to room temperature again or heat gently before serving.)

CHAPTER 4
Deluxe

Rich & indulgent dips

Beetroot hummus

This is a sophisticated dip and dipper combination that's sure to wow party guests. The rich red of the beetroot/beet hummus works beautifully with the dramatic black of the squid ink crackers, and the slightly sweet and salty flavour combination is absolutely stunning.

140 g/1 cup canned chickpeas/ garbanzo beans, drained and rinsed

250 g/2 scant cups beetroot/beets, cooked and cubed

1 large garlic clove, peeled

2 tablespoons olive oil

1 tablespoon freshly squeezed lemon juice

2 tablespoons tahini

2–3 pinches of sea salt flakes

micro herbs such as pea shoots, to garnish

Squid Ink Crackers (see page 137), to serve

SERVES 4–6

To make the hummus, put all of the ingredients in a food processor or blender and blitz until smooth. Taste and adjust the seasoning, if necessary.

Spoon the hummus into a bowl, garnish with a few pea shoots and serve with the Squid Ink Crackers for dipping.

Truffled cauliflower dip

Cauliflower is a hugely versatile and often underrated vegetable. Roasting gives it a delicious nuttiness that balances well here with the richness of truffle oil to make a velvety and indulgent dip.

½ a head of cauliflower, chopped into 1-cm/⅜-in. pieces

vegetable oil, for drizzling

3 tablespoons double/heavy cream or dairy-free substitute if preferred

1 teaspoon truffle oil

salt

6–8 slices thinly sliced toasted sourdough bread, to serve

SERVES 4

Preheat the oven to 180°C (350°F) Gas 4.

Put the cauliflower in a saucepan, cover with water and set over a low–medium heat. Simmer for 5 minutes, then drain and scatter onto a baking sheet. Drizzle the cauliflower with a little vegetable oil and sprinkle with salt. Roast in the oven for 10–12 minutes until just starting to turn golden.

Remove from the oven and return to the saucepan. Add the cream and a pinch of salt. Purée using a hand-held electric/stick blender (or in a blender) until it resembles cottage cheese. Set aside to cool, then put in the refrigerator.

Once the dip has chilled completely, stir in the truffle oil. Serve at room temperature with toasted sourdough.

Roast garlic herbed labneh

Making labneh (also labne, labni or yogurt cheese) is very simple, but do bear in mind that it takes 24 hours to strain the yogurt. Serve this Middle Eastern cheese dip with hot pitta bread or vegetable crudités.

450 g/2 cups full-fat goat's milk yogurt

2 roast garlic cloves (see page 68)

finely grated zest of 1 lemon

3 tablespoons finely chopped fresh flat-leaf parsley

1 teaspoon finely chopped fresh chives

1 teaspoon fresh thyme leaves

salt

TO SERVE

olive oil

pistachio nuts, finely ground

warm pitta bread or vegetable crudités

a muslin/cheesecloth square and string

SERVES 4–6

First, make the labneh. Season the yogurt with salt to taste, mixing it in well. Put the yogurt in the centre of the muslin/cheesecloth square, fold up the muslin around the yogurt and tie tightly, forming a parcel. Suspend the muslin parcel over a deep, large bowl by tying it with string to a wooden spoon laid across the top of the bowl. Leave in the refrigerator for 24 hours, during which time the excess moisture will drip out of the parcel.

Squeeze the roast garlic out of the papery skin and mash into a paste. Flavour the labneh by mixing it with the roast garlic, lemon zest, parsley, chives and thyme.

Transfer the labneh to a dish. Use the back of a spoon to make a little hollow in the middle of the labneh, pour in a little olive oil, sprinkle with ground pistachio nuts and serve with hot pitta bread or vegetable crudités.

Variations

Labneh with dried & fresh mint Beat the labneh with 1 tablespoon of dried mint. Fold in the leaves from a small bunch of fresh mint. Spoon into a bowl and drizzle with good olive oil.

Labneh with garlic, red chillies/chiles & dill Beat the labneh with 1 tablespoon of finely chopped red chilli, 1 crushed garlic clove and 1 tablespoon of finely chopped fresh dill. Spoon into a bowl and garnish with a sprig of dill.

Labneh with harissa, coriander/cilantro & honey Beat the labneh with 2 crushed garlic cloves, ½ teaspoon salt, 2 teaspoons harissa paste, a handful of finely chopped fresh coriander leaves and 1 tablespoon of runny honey. Spoon into a bowl and garnish with a sprig of fresh coriander.

Warm olive & artichoke dip

This is a really savoury and moreish dip with a kick of saltiness from both the olives and Parmesan. Use black olives in place of the green ones, if you prefer them.

160 g/5½ oz. green pitted olives (drained weight), rinsed to remove excess brine

290 g/10 oz. chargrilled artichokes preserved in olive oil, drained

1 tablespoon Worcestershire sauce

1 teaspoon wholegrain mustard

150 ml/5 fl. oz. cup crème fraîche or sour cream

150 g/5½ oz. cream cheese

50 g/2 oz. Parmesan cheese, finely grated

freshly ground black pepper

warm crusty bread, to serve

SERVES 6

Preheat the oven to 180°C (350°F) Gas 4.

Put the drained olives and artichokes in a food processor or blender and blitz until chopped into small pieces.

In a mixing bowl, whisk together the Worcestershire sauce, mustard, crème fraîche and cream cheese until smooth. Reserve a few tablespoons of the grated Parmesan and stir the rest into the mixture. Fold in the chopped artichokes and olives and mix well until everything is coated with the cream cheese mixture. Taste for seasoning – you shouldn't need to add any salt but add black pepper as required.

Spoon into an ovenproof dish and spread out in an even layer. Sprinkle the reserved Parmesan over the top and bake in the preheated oven for 25–30 minutes until the Parmesan starts to turn golden on top. Remove from the oven and leave to cool slightly before serving.

Serve spread onto warm crusty bread.

Saffron lime aïoli with steamed asparagus

A fresh twist on traditional aïoli, the vibrant colours here make a stunning plate of food. If asparagus isn't available, the punchy dip is also delicious with vegetable crudités or fresh crusty bread for dipping.

1 kg/2¼ lb. fresh asparagus, thick stalks removed
1 whole egg and 1 egg yolk
1 teaspoon French mustard
½ teaspoon caster/granulated sugar
1 garlic clove
150 ml/⅔ cup olive oil
2 generous pinches of saffron, soaked in
    1 tablespoon white wine vinegar
grated zest of 1 lime
1 tablespoon lime juice
sea salt and freshly ground black pepper
a handful of freshly snipped chives, to garnish

SERVES 4

Steam the asparagus until tender and refresh with cold water to retain its lovely bright colour.

To make the aïoli, put the egg and egg yolk, mustard, salt, pepper, sugar and garlic into a food processor and whizz, adding the oil little by little until you have a thick mayonnaise.

In a small pan, warm the saffron and vinegar mixture with the lime juice and zest to soften. Cool, then whizz into the mayonnaise.

Serve with the asparagus and snipped chives.

Black olive tapenade

This classic Mediterranean dip is so simple to prepare, it's just a handful of delicious ingredients combined to perfection.

1 garlic clove, crushed
freshly squeezed juice of 1 lemon
3 tablespoons capers, chopped
6 anchovy fillets, chopped
250 g/9 oz. black olives, pitted
leaves from a small bunch of fresh flat-leaf
    parsley, chopped
2–4 tablespoons extra virgin olive oil
salt and freshly ground black pepper
crusty bread and crudités, to serve

SERVES 4

Tip the garlic, lemon juice, capers and anchovy fillets into a food processor and process for about 10 seconds.

Add the olives and parsley and just enough olive oil to make a paste. Season to taste if necessary.

Scrape out into a small bowl and serve with crusty bread and crudités. The dip has a very strong flavour so a little goes a long way!

Whipped garlic potato dip

A wickedly garlicky puréed mashed potato dip, rich with lashings of olive oil that is served at room temperature: be warned, this can become quite addictive! Don't mistake this for a pile of mashed potatoes, it's far richer than that. It can be enjoyed as a dip, best eaten with toasted pitta, but it also works as an accompaniment with grilled fish, meat or vegetables.

400 g/14 oz. potatoes, peeled
½ tablespoon crushed garlic
100 ml/⅓ cup olive oil
freshly squeezed lemon juice, to taste
a pinch of freshly chopped flat-leaf parsley
salt

SERVES 6

Cut the potatoes into large pieces and cook in salted boiling water for about 15–20 minutes, or until there is no resistance when they are pierced with a knife.

Drain and let them steam dry for a few minutes before lightly mashing them. Add the garlic, which should be crushed down to a paste (ideally in a pestle and mortar) and mix through. Start adding the olive oil a little at a time, mashing well between each addition.

Once the potatoes are thoroughly mashed, use a hand whisk to beat them as you add the remaining olive oil and a few drops of lemon juice as you go, just to taste. Season generously with salt and whisk through the parsley.

Roasted red pepper raita

Serve this colourful, cooling dip as part of a summer spread. A spicy lentil chip or cracker works well as a dipper here.

2 red (bell) peppers
1 teaspoon balsamic vinegar
1 teaspoon olive oil
a pinch of salt
400 g/14 oz. Greek/US strained plain yogurt
seeds of ½ a pomegranate
1 teaspoon sumac
spicy lentil crisps/chips or crackers, to serve

SERVES 4–6

Grill/broil or roast the red peppers until they're charred on all sides. Wrap in a plastic bag (which makes them easier to peel afterwards), set aside to cool, then peel, deseed and chop into short strips.

Put the pepper strips in a bowl, add the balsamic vinegar, olive oil and salt and mix together.

Set a few of the pepper strips aside. Fold through the yogurt and stir in most of the pomegranate seeds, but set aside 1 tablespoon to garnish. Stir in ½ teaspoon sumac.

Just before serving, garnish the raita with the reserved pepper strips and pomegranate seeds, and sprinkle over the remaining sumac.

Hot buttered crab dip

Brown crab meat often gets overlooked in favour of fresher-tasting white meat, but it has an incredible richness which makes it a great base for bisques and dips. And it LOVES Amontillado sherry. If you have some crab in the freezer, this is a great dish.

2 tablespoons Amontillado sherry

75 g/⅓ cup unsalted butter, cut into cubes

450 g/1 lb. brown crab meat

2 tablespoons grated Parmesan cheese

a good pinch of mace

cayenne pepper

a squeeze of fresh lemon juice

toast fingers or pitta chips, to serve

SERVES 4

Measure the sherry into a pan and add the cubed butter. Gently melt over a low heat, then stir in the crab meat and Parmesan. Heat through to just under boiling point and simmer for a couple of minutes, then take off the heat and season to taste with mace (go easy, it's powerful), cayenne pepper and a squeeze of lemon. (You probably won't need salt.)

Pour into warmed ramekin dishes, sprinkle lightly with a little more cayenne pepper and serve with toast fingers or pitta chips.

Avocado miso dip with dukkah

This guacamole with a Japanese twist is so quick and easy to make and the Dukkah, an Egyptian nut and spice mix, adds a delicious texture to this snack attack.

120 g/4 oz. avocado, peeled and pitted
1 tablespoon brown rice miso paste
1 tablespoon freshly squeezed lemon juice
2 teaspoons tahini
2 teaspoons extra virgin olive oil
1 small garlic clove, crushed
Vegetable Crisps/Chips (see page 131), to serve

DUKKAH
20 g/2½ tablespoons blanched almonds
20 g/2½ tablespoons blanched hazelnuts
2 tablespoons sesame seeds
1 tablespoon cumin seeds
1 tablespoon coriander seeds
1 tablespoon dried mint

SERVES 2

Preheat the oven to 180°C (350°F) Gas 4.

For the dukkah, roast the almonds in the preheated oven for about 8 minutes, and the hazelnuts for about 5 minutes on separate trays. Leave the nuts to cool.

Meanwhile, in a dry frying pan/skillet over a medium heat, fry the sesame, cumin and coriander seeds for 1–2 minutes until fragrant. In a food processor, blitz the spices, roasted nuts, seeds, dried mint and ¼ teaspoon of sea salt until finely ground, no longer though, as the nuts will begin to release oils. Spoon the mixture into a bowl and set aside.

For the dip, blitz the avocado in the food processor with the miso paste, lemon juice, tahini, olive oil and garlic until smooth. Taste and adjust the seasoning if necessary.

Serve the avocado miso dip with some of the dukkah sprinkled over alongside Vegetable Crisps/Chips. To eat, dunk the chips into the dip and then back into the remaining dukkah, which will cling to the wet dip.

Creamy cashew & roasted tomato dip

This dip has a wonderful nutty texture and the roasted tomatoes give it a sweet, smoky taste This recipe needs some time to prepare as the cashews are best soaked in water overnight so that the dip is creamy.

200 g/7 oz. unsalted cashew nuts, soaked in a bowl of water overnight

250 g/9 oz. sweet cherry tomatoes

1 tablespoon olive oil, plus extra to serve

1 tablespoon balsamic glaze or good-quality balsamic vinegar

1 teaspoon caster/granulated sugar

2 large sprigs of fresh thyme

200 ml/7 fl. oz. buttermilk

freshly squeezed juice of 1 lemon

salt and freshly ground black pepper

Paprika Pitta Chips (see page 132) or crusty bread, to serve

SERVES 4

Preheat the oven to 140°C (275°F) Gas 1.

Cut the tomatoes in half and put, cut-side up, on a roasting pan. Drizzle with the olive oil and balsamic glaze or vinegar and season well with salt and pepper. Sprinkle over the sugar. Pull the thyme sprigs between your fingers to remove the tiny leaves and sprinkle the leaves over the tomatoes. Roast the tomatoes in the preheated oven for about 1½–2 hours, until almost dried but still a little soft. Remove from the oven and leave to cool.

Drain the cashews and discard the water. Put the nuts in a blender with the buttermilk, lemon juice and most of the roasted tomatoes, along with their juices. Reserve a few tomatoes for garnish.

Blitz to a smooth purée and taste for seasoning, adding salt, pepper or lemon juice to taste. Spoon into a bowl and top with the reserved roasted tomatoes and a drizzle of olive oil. Serve with Paprika Pitta Chips or slices of crusty bread for dipping.

Smoked salmon, horseradish & dill dip

Salmon and horseradish are a match made in heaven, and they pair perfectly in this creamy dip. You can adjust the lemon juice to your taste, adding a little more for a really zingy dip.

200 g/7 oz. smoked salmon slices

freshly squeezed juice of 1 lemon

250 ml/1 cup crème fraîche or
   sour cream

1 tablespoon fresh dill, chopped,
   plus extra to serve

125 g/4½ oz. cream cheese

1 tablespoon creamed horseradish

freshly ground black pepper

Bagel Toasts (see page 133),
   warmed, to serve

SERVES 4

Reserve a piece of smoked salmon for garnish, then blitz the rest into small pieces in a food processor or blender with the lemon juice. Add the crème fraîche, dill, cream cheese and creamed horseradish and season with freshly ground black pepper. Smoked salmon is quite salty so you shouldn't need to add salt. Blitz for a few seconds until everything is combined.

Spoon into a bowl and garnish with the reserved salmon and some more dill sprigs.

Serve the dip with warm Bagel Toasts on the side.

Variation: Smoked salmon, caper & red onion dip
Try replacing the dill and horseradish with a few spoonfuls of drained and chopped capers and some very finely chopped red onion.

Lime butter dip *with lobster tails*

This is a recipe for a special occasion. It's a good idea to make friends with your fishmonger who can cut the lobster tails in half for you.

5 tablespoons freshly squeezed lime juice

150 g/1¼ sticks unsalted butter

2 raw large lobster tails, cut in half

1 tablespoon olive oil

sea salt and freshly ground black pepper

2 limes cut into wedges, to serve

crusty bread, to serve

SERVES 4

Preheat the oven to 200°C (400°F) Gas 6. Warm a baking sheet in the oven.

Heat the lime juice in a medium-sized saucepan. Add the butter and whisk to form a sauce.

Season the lobster tails with salt and pepper. Heat the oil in a large frying pan/skillet and fry the lobster tails for 3 minutes. Transfer them to the hot baking sheet, drizzle with half of the lime butter and roast in the preheated oven for 10 minutes until the flesh is opaque.

Serve the lobster tails with lime wedges, a pot of the remaining lime butter for dipping and crusty bread to mop up any juices.

Smoked 'ahi dip

If you can't get your hands on smoked 'ahi fish, you can use cooked tuna with a few drops of smoked paprika to give it that lovely smoky taste.

400 g/14 oz. smoked 'ahi
2 tablespoons freshly squeezed lemon juice
3 tablespoons mayonnaise
dash of Worcestershire sauce
dash of Tabasco sauce
3 tablespoons freshly chopped chives, plus extra to garnish
1 tablespoon very finely diced shallot (optional)
pinch of Old Bay Seasoning (optional)
sea salt and freshly ground black pepper

TO SERVE
Homemade Tortilla Chips (see page 132)
vegetable crudités
lemon or lime wedges

SERVES 4

Using your hands or a fork, flake the fish. Place all the ingredients into a bowl (or use a food processor). Mix to a smooth but textured consistency, ensuring there are no big chunks.

Garnish with extra chives and serve with tortilla chips or crudités and some lemon or lime wedges.

Tip: For a more substantial snack, serve as a pâté on toast. You can also use pretty much any smoked fish (smoked marlin or swordfish work well), adding more or less sour cream according to your preference. Jazz up with capers, diced (bell) pepper or chopped gherkin.

Guacamame dip

Similar to guacamole, but with added protein from the edamame beans, this fresh dip works beautifully served with the Smoked 'Ahi Dip (left) or any rich fish or seafood dip.

1 ripe avocado
freshly squeezed juice of 2 limes
350 g/12 oz. edamame beans, shelled (defrosted if frozen)
1 tablespoon finely chopped red onion
2 tablespoons finely chopped tomato
handful of fresh coriander/cilantro, finely chopped
½ red chilli/chile, deseeded and chopped (optional)
¼ teaspoon each sea salt and freshly ground black pepper

SERVES 4–6

Slice the avocado in half lengthways and remove the pit. Scoop the flesh into a bowl, mash with a fork and sprinkle with the lime juice. Put all the remaining ingredients in a food processor and blitz for a minute or two to a smooth, creamy consistency. Gently stir this mixture with the avocado. Taste and season, adding extra salt, lime juice or chilli as necessary.

Cover and pop in the fridge for 20 minutes to help the dip chill and set, or serve immediately.

Tip: Garnish the dip with some chopped coriander, edamame beans or sliced red chilli.

Blue cheese fondue with walnut grissini, grapes & asparagus

Blue cheese and fresh walnuts make a delicious combination. This fondue is perfect served as an appetizer with grissini, grapes and asparagus. Alternatively, try serving this fondue as a dessert course with ripe pears, cut into quarters for dipping.

125 ml/½ cup sweet white wine, such as German Riesling or Gewürztraminer

400 g/14 oz. creamy blue cheese, such as Gorgonzola or Roquefort, coarsely chopped

1 teaspoon cornflour/cornstarch, mixed with 1 tablespoon of the wine

TO SERVE
Walnut Grissini (see page 136)
black grapes
asparagus spears, lightly cooked,

SERVES 6

To prepare the fondue, pour the wine into the fondue pot and heat until simmering on the stovetop.

Gradually stir in the blue cheese, then the cornflour mixture, stirring constantly until smooth.

Transfer the pot to its tabletop burner and serve with Walnut Grissini, grapes and asparagus.

CHAPTER 5
Dirty

Fast food-inspired crowd-pleasers

Hot Philly steak dip

This recipe is inspired by one of the most popular steak recipes in America – a Philly cheesesteak – a steak sandwich made with thin slices of beef, topped with melting cheese. Dip in tortilla chips or crusty bread while watching the Super Bowl.

1 green (bell) pepper

1 medium onion

1 tablespoon olive oil

1 teaspoon balsamic glaze or vinegar

1 teaspoon caster/granulated sugar

6 slices roast beef

250 g/9 oz. cream cheese

125 ml/½ cup your favourite ranch salad dressing

1 tablespoon creamed horseradish

100 g/3½ oz. provolone or Cheddar cheese, grated

salt and freshly ground black pepper

tortilla chips (shop-bought or see page 132) or crusty bread, to serve

SERVES 6–8

Preheat the oven to 180°C (350°F) Gas 4.

Cut away the top of the green pepper and discard. Cut the pepper in half, remove all of the seeds, then cut into small chunks about 1-cm/½-in. diameter. Peel and finely chop the onion. Put the peppers and onion in a large frying pan/skillet with the olive oil and fry over a gentle heat until the onions and peppers are soft and the onion starts to caramelize. Drizzle with the balsamic, sprinkle over the caster/granulated sugar, season with salt and pepper and fry/sauté for a few more minutes.

Cut the roast beef into small pieces and add to the pan. Cook for a minute or so, for the meat to absorb the flavours from the pan. Remove from the heat and leave to cool for a few minutes.

In a mixing bowl, whisk together the cream cheese, ranch dressing and creamed horseradish. Fold the grated cheese into the mixture with the beef and vegetables.

Bake in the preheated oven for 20–25 minutes until the cheese has melted and the top of the dip has started to turn light golden brown. Leave to cool for about 10 minutes before serving, as the dip should be served warm and not hot. Serve with tortilla chips or small slices of crusty bread for dipping. Delicious!

Variation: Spicy hot Philly dip To make a spicy version, fold in some finely chopped jarred jalapeños with the beef before baking.

Hawaiian-style bacon & pineapple dip

This decadent hot dip is made with gooey melted cheese, pineapple and salty pancetta. You can replace the pancetta with ready-cooked ham or fried bacon lardons if you prefer. Or, if pepperoni pizza is your favourite, try swapping the pancetta for pepperoni slices. Fresh pineapple is usually best as it has more flavour, but canned pineapple is also fine to use and is quicker to prepare.

100 g/3½ oz. pancetta rashers/ slices

4 slices of fresh pineapple or 4 canned pineapple rings

250 g/9 oz. cream cheese

125 ml/½ cup your favourite Thousand Island dressing

1 tablespoon sun-dried tomato purée/paste

100 g/3½ oz. Red Leicester or Colby cheese, grated

salt and freshly ground black pepper

Homemade Tortilla Chips (see page 132) or crusty bread, to serve

SERVES 6–8

Preheat the oven to 180°C (350°F) Gas 4.

Chop the strips of pancetta into about 3-cm/1-in. pieces and put in the roasting pan.

If using a fresh pineapple, remove the skin, eyes and hard core, then chop into small pieces. If using canned pineapple, chop the rings into small pieces.

Add the pineapple to the roasting pan and bake in the hot oven for 10 minutes. Remove from the oven and leave to cool slightly.

Put the cream cheese in a mixing bowl. Add the Thousand Island dressing and tomato purée and whisk together until smooth. Stir in the grated cheese, cooled pancetta and pineapple pieces, and season with salt and pepper. Bake in the preheated oven for 20–25 minutes until golden brown on top. Leave to cool slightly for about 10 minutes, then serve warm with Homemade Tortilla Crisps/Chips or crusty bread for dipping.

Variation: Hawaiian 'pizza' dip Try using pepperoni slices instead of the pancetta and arrange them on top of the dip as you would with a pizza. To reinforce the theme, you can serve it with a pizza dough base, cut into wedges for dipping.

Spicy chilli bean dip

Shiny, kidney-shaped black beans are especially popular in Latin American cooking. They are left whole in this recipe, but you could roughly mash after cooking to make the dip more gooey.

440 g/2 cups dried black beans

2 tablespoons olive oil

1 red onion, chopped

4 garlic cloves, chopped

1 red (bell) pepper, deseeded and diced

1 tablespoon ground cumin

2 teaspoons dried Greek oregano

2 teaspoons chilli/chili powder

2 x 400-g/14-oz. cans chopped tomatoes

a handful of fresh coriander/ cilantro leaves, chopped

Greek yogurt, to serve

warmed corn chips, to serve

SERVES 6–8

Put the dried beans in a saucepan with 2 litres/quarts cold water. Bring to the boil, then reduce the heat to a low simmer and cook the beans, uncovered, for about 1½ hours, until just tender and not falling apart. Drain well and set aside.

Heat the oil in a large, heavy-based saucepan set over a medium heat. When the oil is hot, add the onion, garlic and pepper and cook for 8–10 minutes, until softened. Stir in the cumin, oregano and chilli powder and fry for 1 minute.

Increase the heat to high. Add the tomatoes, beans and 250 ml/ 1 cup cold water and bring to the boil. Reduce the heat to low, partially cover the pan and cook for 1½–2 hours, adding a little more water from time to time if the mixture is drying or catching on the bottom of the pan.

Transfer the dip to a serving bowl and serve with the yogurt, coriander on top and corn chips for dipping.

Spicy beer mustard dip
with maple-glazed sausages

This delicious mustard dip is classically served with soft pretzels or sausages. Here it's paired with little cocktail sausages, which are the ideal size for dipping! Making your own mustard is easy, although you will need to soak the mustard seeds overnight.

80 g/3 oz. yellow mustard seeds
25 g/1 oz. black mustard seeds
125 ml/½ cup strong beer
125 ml/½ cup cider vinegar
80 g/½ cup soft dark brown sugar
40 ml/2½ tablespoons maple syrup
1 teaspoon ground allspice
1 tablespoon creamed horseradish
salt and freshly ground black
    pepper

Maple-glazed sausages
24 mini sausages or 12 chipolatas
12 rashers/slices streaky bacon
a little olive oil
3 tablespoons maple syrup
1 tablespoon sesame seeds

cocktail sticks/toothpicks

SERVES 6–8

Put the yellow and black mustard seeds in a bowl and pour over the beer and cider vinegar. Cover the bowl with clingfilm/plastic wrap and put in the refrigerator overnight to soak. The mustard seeds will absorb some of the liquid and become soft.

The following day, put the soaked seeds and soaking liquor into a food processor or blender with the sugar, maple syrup, ground allspice and creamed horseradish and blitz for a few minutes until smooth. It will still have some small pieces of mustard seed which give a great texture to the dip. Season with salt and pepper to your taste. This recipe makes plenty of mustard, so you may want to reserve half in a sealed jar and keep it in the refrigerator.

For the sausages, preheat the oven to 180°C (350°F) Gas 4.

If using chipolatas, twist the centre of each sausage then cut with scissors to make 24 mini sausages. Cut the bacon strips in half, wrap one half strip around each mini sausage and secure in place with a cocktail stick/toothpick. Put in a roasting pan and drizzle with a little olive oil and roast in the oven for 25–30 minutes until the sausages turn golden brown. Drizzle with the maple syrup, sprinkle with the sesame seeds and bake for a further 5 minutes. Serve the sausages hot or cold with the spicy beer mustard dip.

Hot buffalo chicken wing dip

This dip has the taste of hot buffalo wings but without the bother of getting messy fingers eating actual wings. Hot sauces vary in strength, so add gradually and taste to ensure you don't end up with a dip that is too hot.

300 g/10½ oz. cream cheese
170 ml/¾ cup ranch salad dressing
125 ml/½ cup red hot chilli sauce (such as Frank's)
150 g/5½ oz. Cheddar cheese, grated
200 g/7 oz. cooked chicken breast
freshly ground black pepper
tortilla chips (shop-bought or homemade, see page 132), to serve

SERVES 6–8

Preheat the oven to 180°C (350°F) Gas 4.

Put the cream cheese, ranch dressing and hot sauce in a bowl and whisk together until smooth. Stir in the grated cheese. Remove any skin from the chicken breasts and discard, then chop into small pieces and stir into the sauce. Season with ground black pepper and taste. You can add a little salt if you wish, but there should be sufficient salt from the dressing and hot sauce.

Bake in the preheated oven for 25–30 minutes until the top of the dip starts to turn light golden brown. Remove from the oven and leave to cool for a short while, then serve warm with tortilla chips.

Variation: Vegetarian buffalo 'chicken wing' dip To make a version suitable for vegetarians to enjoy, simply use a vegetarian cheese and replace the cooked chicken breast with butter/lima beans or small florets of steamed or boiled cauliflower.

Tuna melt dip

The tried-and-tested combination of tuna and melted Cheddar creates a hot dip that's sure to become a family favourite.

225 g/8 oz. cream cheese
2 tablespoons butter, softened
2 tablespoons mayonnaise
65 ml/½ cup sour cream
2 tablespoons freshly squeezed lemon juice
1–2 tablespoons very finely diced spring onions/scallions
2 tablespoons chopped fresh flat-leaf parsley
½ teaspoon paprika
¼ teaspoon ground black pepper
2 x 400-g/14 oz. cans tuna, drained
50 g/½ cup grated Cheddar cheese
Homemade Classic Potato Crisps/Chips (see page 136), to serve

SERVES 6–8

Preheat the oven to 180°C (350°F) Gas 4.

Blend the cream cheese with the softened butter. Blend in the mayonnaise and sour cream until smooth. Add the lemon juice, spring onion, parsley, paprika and pepper. Stir in the flaked, well-drained tuna and cheese.

Bake in the preheated oven for 10–15 minutes, until hot and bubbly. Remove from the oven and leave to cool for 10 minutes before serving with Homemade Classic Potato Crisps.

Layered 'nacho' dip *with tortilla chips*

One of the all-time favourite sharing plates is nachos – tortilla chips are served piled high with tomato salsa, guacamole, sour cream and grated cheese, then warmed under a grill/broiler. This dip version is layered up in a bowl and then warmed, ready to scoop out with crunchy tortilla chips.

GUACAMOLE

6 ripe avocados, halved and pitted

½ red onion

a handful of freshly chopped coriander/cilantro

2 fresh red chillies/chiles, deseeded and finely chopped

freshly squeezed juice of 2 limes

2–3 pinches of sea salt flakes

Tabasco and cayenne pepper (optional), to taste

TOMATO SALSA

6 ripe medium tomatoes

freshly squeezed juice of 1 lime

10g/⅓ oz. fresh coriander/cilantro

2 spring onions/scallions, trimmed

1 fresh red chilli/chile, trimmed and deseeded

salt and freshly ground black pepper

TO ASSEMBLE

200 ml/7 fl. oz. sour cream

125 g/4½ oz. strong cheese, such as mature/sharp Cheddar, grated

a handful of jarred jalapeño slices (optional)

Homemade Tortilla Chips (see page 132), to serve

SERVES 6

Scoop the flesh out of the avocados with a tablespoon into a shallow bowl. Add the onion, coriander and chillies. Add the lime juice, then mash everything together with a fork, leaving the texture quite chunky. Season with salt to taste. Add a few dashes of Tabasco and a few pinches of cayenne, if using. Cover with clingfilm/plastic wrap until ready to use.

For the salsa, cut the tomatoes in half then scoop out and discard the seeds. Put in a blender or food processor along with the lime juice, coriander, spring onions and chilli and pulse for a few seconds to roughly chop the tomatoes. Season to taste with salt and pepper. Cover with clingfilm until ready to use.

To assemble the dip, spoon the guacamole into a shallow serving bowl and spread out in a thick layer. Top with the tomato salsa, then spoon over the sour cream, scatter over the grated cheese and finish with jalapeños, if using. Gently warm under a preheated grill/broiler just until the cheese starts to melt. Serve straight away with the tortilla chips.

Spicy rémoulade dip with southern-style crab fritters

These Deep South-style crab fritters are perfect for sharing. Just make sure you make enough of the spicy rémoulade dip to go around!

250 ml/1 cup mayonnaise

1 tablespoon Dijon mustard

1 tablespoon tomato ketchup

1 garlic clove, crushed

1 tablespoon paprika

1 teaspoon hot sauce, such as Tabasco

2 tablespoons capers, coarsely chopped

a small squeeze of fresh lemon juice

¼ teaspoon salt

SOUTHERN-STYLE CRAB FRITTERS

2 x 145-g/5¼-oz. cans lump crab meat

1 tablespoons capers, coarsely chopped

a few sprigs of fresh dill and flat-leaf parsley, chopped

1 teaspoon Worcestershire sauce

a pinch of salt

1 egg

150 g/3 cups fresh breadcrumbs

vegetable oil, for shallow frying

MAKES 12

Start by making the spicy dip; mix all the ingredients together and taste, adding a little more of any of the ingredients to your taste. Set aside.

To make the fritters, place the crab meat in a sieve/strainer and gently push down to extract the excess liquid, then leave to drain.

Place the capers, herbs, Worcestershire sauce, salt and egg in a mixing bowl, add 4 tablespoons of the spicy rémoulade sauce and whisk together, ensuring the egg is all fully incorporated. Fold in one-third of the breadcrumbs and all the crab meat, trying not to over-mix.

Place the remaining breadcrumbs in a flat dish. Take a ping-pong ball-sized portion of the crab mixture, roll into a ball between the palms of your hands and then flatten a little (the mixture will be slightly wet which is perfect for coating in the remaining breadcrumbs). Roll the ball in the breadcrumbs, coating it on all sides. Repeat with the remaining mixture to make 12 fritters.

Heat enough vegetable oil to coat the bottom of a saucepan. Fry the fritters for 2–4 minutes on each side until golden (you may need to cook them in batches to avoid over-crowding the pan). Remove from the pan and set on paper towels to drain. Season with a pinch of salt and transfer to a serving dish with the remaining spicy rémoulade dip on the side.

Blue cheese, garlic & thyme dip with potato fries & pickled red onion rings

Blue cheese with fries is an all-time delicious combination, and the pickled red onion rings add just the right amount of acidity to cut through the richness. For this recipe it's best to use a mild blue cheese such as the blended cheese Cambozola, a Danish blue or Gorgonzola.

250 g/9 oz. Cambozola, diced
200 g/7 oz. Gruyère, grated
1 tablespoon white vinegar
1 tablespoon cornflour/cornstarch
1 tablespoon olive oil
1 garlic clove, crushed
1 teaspoon freshly chopped thyme
150 ml/⅔ cup light blonde beer
3 tablespoons single/light cream
salt and freshly ground black
   pepper

PICKLED RED ONION RINGS
125 ml/½ cup cider vinegar
30 g/2½ tablespoons granulated
   sugar
1 teaspoon salt
1 red onion, thinly sliced
1 garlic clove, thinly sliced
a pinch of black peppercorns

POTATO FRIES
1 kg/2 lb. 4 oz. Maris Piper, Yukon
   Gold or King Edward potatoes
1 tablespoon olive oil

TO SERVE
chargrilled bread or Little Gem/
   Boston lettuce quarters
ripe pear wedges

SERVES 6

First make the pickled onion rings. Place the vinegar, 125 ml/ ½ cup water, the sugar and salt in a small saucepan and bring to the boil over a low heat. Let it boil for 1 minute, then remove from the heat. Meanwhile, place the onion, garlic and peppercorns into a sterilized 350-ml/12-oz. jar. Pour the hot pickling mixture directly over the onion and seal the jar with a vinegar-safe lid. Cool and set aside until required.

Preheat the oven to 200°C (400°F) Gas 6 and line a large baking sheet with baking paper.

Cut the potatoes into thin fries, no more than 5 mm/¼ in. thick and place on the prepared baking sheet. Add the oil, salt and pepper and stir well. Bake in the oven for 45–50 minutes, stirring from time to time, until crisp and golden.

Meanwhile, combine the cheeses with a little pepper. Stir the vinegar and cornflour/cornstarch together until smooth. About 10 minutes before the potatoes are cooked, heat the oil in a fondue pot on the stovetop and gently fry the garlic and thyme over a low heat for 3 minutes until softened. Add the beer and cream and bring to the boil, then stir in the cheese until melted. Stir in the cornflour and vinegar mixture and simmer for about 1–2 minutes until thickened.

Arrange the potato fries on plates or in bowls and serve with the dip and pickled onion rings.

Quick chilli lime mayo

This is a hot and fruity mayonnaise that literally takes seconds to make. It's great with any seafood and does wonders for a posh tuna sandwich!

4 tablespoons mayonnaise
grated zest and freshly
squeezed juice of 1 small lime
1 Scotch Bonnet chilli/chile,
very finely chopped

MAKES 4 TABLESPOONS

Mix the mayonnaise and lime juice in a small bowl. Add the Scotch Bonnet, little by little, until the desired hotness is achieved. Garnish with lime zest.

Fresh aïoli

This popular dip is lovely with potatoes or anything barbecued/grilled, especially prawns/shrimp or chicken. This recipe has a wonderful, robust garlicky flavour, not for the faint-hearted.

2 large egg yolks
4 very fresh garlic cloves,
crushed
1 teaspoon Dijon mustard
150 ml/⅔ cup good-quality
light olive oil
freshly squeezed juice of
½ lemon
sea salt and freshly ground
black pepper

MAKES ABOUT 200 ML/¾ CUP

Beat the eggs yolks in a large bowl with a balloon whisk. Add the garlic and mustard and beat through. While beating the mixture, slowly add the olive oil in a thin, steady stream. When all the oil has been added, the aïoli should have a smooth, velvety appearance. Add the lemon juice, season with salt and pepper and gently stir through. Refrigerate until ready to serve.

Roast garlic & chipotle mayo

This tasty mayonnaise is really big on flavour. It's just right for alternative egg mayonnaise sandwiches or an amazing potato salad.

2 large garlic cloves, skin on
4 tablespoons mayonnaise
½ teaspoon crushed chipotle
chilli

MAKES 4 TABLESPOONS

Preheat the oven to 180°C (350°F) Gas 4.

Roast the garlic on a baking sheet in the preheated oven for 20 minutes until soft but not burnt. Remove from the oven and let cool for 10 minutes. Squeeze the garlic from its skin into a small bowl. Gently mash with a fork. Add the mayonnaise and chipotle and stir until evenly mixed. Cover and refrigerate for 2–3 hours to let the chipotle rehydrate a little in the mayonnaise. Stir occasionally while it's chilling.

CHAPTER 6

Dippers

Vegetable crisps/chips

These no-fry veggie crisps/chips require a little effort in the kitchen, but they are so much more special than your average store-bought potato crisp/chip. Made from highly nutritious root vegetables, they are bursting with earthy, complex flavours to take your dipping game to the next level. Do not expect them to be as crunchy as deep-fried crisps/chips, but their amazingly rich taste will compensate for that.

400 g/3 large carrots
400 g/2 large beetroots/beets
   (you can use regular or a mix
   of golden or candied)
400 g/3 large parsnips
3 tablespoons olive oil
1 teaspoon fine sea salt

dehydrator

MAKES ABOUT 4–6 SERVINGS

Scrub all the root vegetables well and remove the tops and any black spots. Using a mandoline, slice them lengthways to get the longest strips possible. Small pieces will shrink into bite-size crisps/chips. Also, the slices should not be see-through thin.

Place in separate bowls and add 1 tablespoon of oil and a pinch of salt to each batch. Mix thoroughly.

Place on dehydrator trays in a single layer and dehydrate for 2 hours on maximum temperature, then lower the temperature to 50°C/100°F and dehydrate for another 5 hours, or until crispy.

Homemade tortilla chips

The ultimate dipper, perfect for serving with all manner of dips and snacks.

8 small soft wheat flour tortillas
sunflower or vegetable oil, for frying

SERVES 6

Stack the tortillas and cut each one into 8 even triangles, like a pizza.

Pour about 2.5 cm/1 in. oil into a small saucepan, then put over a medium-high heat.

When the oil is hot, you can test-fry one tortilla triangle – it should take about 30 seconds for the first side to become crisp.

Using tongs or a slotted spoon, turn the tortilla over to fry the other side.

Fry the remaining tortillas in batches and, when golden brown, drain on paper towels.

When cool, store in an airtight container until ready to use.

Paprika pitta chips

A little added seasoning elevates these crispy chips and makes them a perfect partner for any creamy dips.

2 tablespoons olive oil
1 tablespoon smoked paprika
5 white pitta breads, halved lengthways and cut into strips
salt and freshly ground black pepper

SERVES 4–6

Preheat the oven to 200°C (400°F) Gas 6.

Drizzle a foil-lined baking sheet with the olive oil, then sprinkle over the paprika and some salt and black pepper.

Put the pitta bread strips on the baking sheet and mix to coat in the oil and seasoning.

Bake in the preheated oven for 8 minutes until slightly coloured and crisp.

Herby breadsticks

This long, crispy breadstick with the addition of mixed dried herbs is delightful served with hummus or a melted cheese fondue dip.

300 g/2¼ cups plain/all-purpose flour
2 teaspoons fast-action yeast
2 teaspoons salt
1 teaspoon sugar
4 tablespoons/¼ cup olive oil
120–150 ml/½–⅔ cup lukewarm water
a pinch of mixed dried herbs
a pinch of cayenne pepper
salt and freshly ground black pepper

SERVES 4–6

Preheat the oven to 170°C (325°F) Gas 3.

Combine the flour, yeast, salt and sugar in a bowl. Make a well in the centre, pour in the olive oil and water, and stir until well combined and the dough comes together. It should be soft but not sticky.

Knead the dough for 10 minutes by hand, cover with oiled clingfilm/plastic wrap or a damp cloth and leave it to rise in a warm place for 40–60 minutes, or until doubled in size.

Divide the dough in half and keep half wrapped up so that it does not dry out. Roll half the dough out into a flat rectangle about 5 mm–1 cm/¼–⅜ in. thick, then cut it into 1-cm/⅜-in.-wide strips. Roll the strips into pencil-width tubes. Repeat with the other half of the dough.

Spread the mixed dried herbs, cayenne pepper and salt and pepper on a board, then roll the breadsticks in them and put them on a floured baking sheet. Bake in the preheated oven for 20–30 minutes until golden. Remove from the oven and let cool on a wire rack.

Bagel toasts

Bagel toasts work really well and are so simple to make, there's no comparison between shop-bought and homemade.

3 plain bagels, stale is fine!
3 tablespoons olive oil
1 tablespoon poppy seeds or sesame seeds (optional)

SERVES 4

Preheat the grill/broiler to hot.

Using a sharp knife, slice each bagel horizontally into 4 and arrange the thin slices on the grill pan.

Grill on one side until lightly browned, then remove from the oven and turn over.

Brush the oil over the untoasted side of the bagels. Scatter over the seeds, if using, and return to the grill/broiler. Toast until crisp and golden.

Serve immediately or let cool and store in an airtight container for up to 2 days.

Grissini

Crunchy homemade grissini are delicious on their own, but pairing them with a tasty dip for a snack or an easy appetizer is a great idea. Sesame seeds are added into the grissini dough here to give these breadsticks a beautifully nutty taste.

140 ml /²⁄₃ cup lukewarm water

5 g/scant 2 teaspoons active dry yeast

5 g/1 teaspoon barley malt (or agave syrup)

190 g/1½ cup unbleached plain/all-purpose flour

60 g/½ cup wholemeal/whole-wheat flour

4 g/scant 1 teaspoon salt

2 tablespoons raw, unhulled sesame seeds, plus 1 tablespoon extra for sprinkling

3 tablespoons light sesame or olive oil

MAKES 20 GRISSINI

In a small bowl, combine the water with the yeast and malt. Whisk and let sit for 15 minutes. The yeast will start to foam lightly.

In a separate bowl, combine the flours, salt, sesame seeds and 2 tablespoons of the oil. Stir in the bubbly yeast mixture and knead until smooth; about 4 minutes. Place on a baking sheet lined with baking parchment. With the help of a silicone spatula, oil the dough lightly. Let rise in the oven with only the light on, for 1 hour.

Preheat the oven to 180°C (350°F) Gas 4.

Form the dough into an oval shape and, with the help of a sharp wide knife, cut 1-cm/⅜-in. strips of dough. Stretch each strip with your fingers into a long grissino; some strips will be longer and thicker, so you'll be able to stretch two or three grissini out of them. From this amount of dough, you should get 20 grissini (35 cm/14 in. long and 1 cm/⅜ in. thick). They do puff a little while baking in the oven.

Place the stretched grissini on a second baking sheet lined with baking parchment, 7 mm/¼ in. apart. Brush with the remaining oil and sprinkle with the extra sesame seeds. Bake in the preheated oven for 12–15 minutes in two batches, rotating them halfway through. Let cool and serve with any dip. If any are leftover, store in a sealable bag at room temperature.

Homemade classic potato crisps/chips

You can't beat a good homemade potato crisp/chip for dipping and snacking on. Feel free to add different seasonings to change things up too.

800 g/1¾ lb. small waxy fingerling potatoes, such as Anya, Pink Fir Apple or Kipfler, cut into 3-mm/⅛-in. thick slices
125 ml/½ cup olive oil
125 ml/½ cup vegetable oil

SERVES 6

Bring a large saucepan of lightly salted water to the boil. Add the potatoes, cover the pan and remove from the heat. Leave in the hot water for 5 minutes. Drain well and arrange the slices on a wire rack in a single layer until completely cool.

Put the oils in a saucepan or large frying pan/skillet set over a high heat. When the oil is hot, cook the potato slices in batches for 5–6 minutes each, turning once or twice, until crisp and golden.

Remove from the oil using a metal slotted spoon and drain on paper towels.

Walnut grissini

A variation on the Grissini on page 134, these have a strong taste of walnuts and are perfect with cheesy dips and hummus.

375 g/generous 2¾ cups unbleached plain/all-purpose flour, plus extra for dusting
1 sachet (7 g/¼ oz.) easy-blend dried yeast
70 g/2½ oz. fresh walnuts
1 teaspoon sea salt
2 tablespoons walnut oil

SERVES 6

Put the flour, yeast, walnuts and salt into a food processor fitted with a plastic blade. With the machine running, add the oil and 200 ml/¾ cup water through the feed tube. Process in 15-second bursts until it forms a soft mass.

Turn out onto a floured board and knead for 2 minutes. Put the dough into a lightly oiled bowl, cover and let rest for 1 hour.

Preheat the oven to 200°C (400°F) Gas 6.

Knead the dough again lightly, flatten to a rectangle about 40 x 15 cm/16 x 6 in., then cut crossways into 1-cm/½-in. strips. Roll and stretch out each strip to about 30 cm/12 in. in length and transfer to a baking sheet (you will need to bake in two batches).

Bake in the preheated oven for 16–18 minutes. Remove from the oven and let cool on a wire rack.

Serve immediately or store in an airtight container for up to 1 week.

Squid ink crackers

These deluxe crackers will add a flair of class to any mezze dip selection. The squid ink is available in convenient sachets from Italian and Spanish specialist grocery stores, and from some online retailers.

300 g/2¼ cups plain/all-purpose flour
1 teaspoon baking powder
1 teaspoon salt
½ teaspoon cayenne pepper
80 ml/⅓ cup olive oil
3 x 4 g/⅙ oz. squid ink sachets

SERVES 4–6

Preheat the oven to 180°C (350°F) Gas 4.

Mix the flour, baking powder, salt and cayenne pepper in a large mixing bowl, and make a well in the middle. Mix 150 ml/⅔ cup water with the olive oil and squid ink, then add to the well. Stir gently, slowly incorporating the dry ingredients until a dough forms.

Turn out the dough onto a floured surface, and knead for about 3–5 minutes, or until smooth. Divide the dough into 15 pieces and roll them into the desired shapes with a rolling pin.

Transfer the shapes to a baking sheet lined with baking parchment and bake in the preheated oven for about 10–15 minutes, or until crisp on the undersides. Cool on a wire rack.

Keep in an airtight container for up to 3 days before serving.

Crostini

Crispy crostini work wonderfully for dipping and also for topping with paté or spreads.

2 wholemeal/wholewheat baguettes/French sticks, each sliced into 30–35 slices about 5 mm/¼ in. thick
100 ml/scant ½ cup olive oil

SERVES 4–6

Heat a griddle pan/grill pan over a high heat and brush each side of the bread with olive oil.

Cook the bread, in batches, for 1 minute on each side, until the bread is toasted and crisp. Remove and put onto a wire rack to cool.

Alternatively, bake them on a baking sheet in an oven at 180°C (350°F) Gas 4 for 8–10 minutes.

Red pepper & buckwheat crackers

The ingredients list for these crackers might look a bit unusual, as they don't include any flour and raw veggies go directly into the dough, but give this recipe a chance and you'll discover how healthy ingredients can also make delicious crackers! If you have health-conscious foodies coming over for dinner or a snack, these are a great choice.

270 g/1½ cups buckwheat, soaked in water overnight and well drained

5 tablespoons flax or chia seeds, soaked in water, plus extra for sprinkling

½ teaspoon sea salt

100 g/1 medium red (bell) pepper, topped, tailed and deseeded

60 g/½ cup chopped onion

1 tablespoon sweet paprika

¼ teaspoon smoked sweet paprika, plus extra for sprinkling

110 ml/½ cup pure carrot juice or water

MAKES 12–16 CRACKERS

In a high-speed blender, blend all the ingredients into a thick, smooth paste.

Cut a piece of baking parchment to the size of your oven rack/ baking pan and place it on a smooth surface (kitchen counter or table). Spoon the cracker paste onto the baking parchment and spread to get a rectangle-shaped even surface. If you like really crunchy crackers, the dough should be almost paper-thin, but if you like a bit of texture, roll to desired thickness. Sprinkle the dough evenly with extra soaked flax or chia seeds and a couple of pinches of smoked sweet paprika.

Put the oven rack/baking pan on the edge of the counter and quickly pull the baking parchment with the cracker paste to slide onto it. Place in the top of the oven; turn on the fan and the heat up to 100°C (200°F). Prop the door open with a folded kitchen towel, to ensure proper dehydration. Dehydrate for 2–3 hours.

Check the cracker dough and, if it isn't sticky, peel off the baking parchment and break into your desired shapes. Further dehydrate the crackers directly on the oven rack until dried. If you have a dehydrator, you could always use that instead. Store the crackers in a sealable bag in the fridge.

Rye crackers with chia seeds

You can either use these crackers for dipping after they've cooled down, or spread any dip you have over them, top that with veggies or other toppings of your choice and munch your worries away!

130 g/¾ cup rye flour

130 g/¾ cup unbleached plain/
   all-purpose flour

15 g/2 tablespoons chia seeds

4 g/scant 1 teaspoon salt

freshly ground black pepper,
   to taste

60 ml/¼ cup olive oil or light
   sesame oil

60 ml/¼ cup water

1 teaspoon dark agave or maple
   syrup

hummus, cucumber and micro
   cress, to serve (optional)

MAKES 12–16 CRACKERS

Combine all the dry ingredients in a large bowl. Emulsify all the wet ingredients with a whisk, and then slowly add them to the flour and seed mixture, stirring until well combined. The dough should quickly form a ball and shouldn't be sticky. Knead a couple of times; just enough to make sure all the ingredients are evenly distributed. Wrap in clingfilm/plastic wrap and let sit at room temperature for 10 minutes. Resting the dough makes rolling it out much easier.

Preheat the oven to 200°C (400°F) Gas 6.

Divide the dough into three equal pieces. Roll out a very thin layer of dough between two sheets of baking parchment. If you like really crunchy crackers, the dough should be almost paper-thin, but if you like a bit of texture, roll to desired thickness.

Use a knife or pizza cutter to cut out shapes. Squares or rectangles are practical choices, since you'll have not much leftover dough. Transfer the crackers to a baking sheet lined with baking parchment using a thin spatula or a knife. Prick each a couple of times with a fork.

Bake in the preheated oven for 4–7 minutes, depending on the thickness of the crackers. Remember, they shouldn't brown, just get slightly golden. They will firm up as they cool, so don't expect them to be cracker-crunchy straight out of the oven.

Here, they are spread with hummus and topped with cucumber and micro cress, but you can eat them how you prefer! Store in an air-tight container after they've cooled completely.

Index

Recipe Credits

Ghillie Başan
Zhug

Fiona Beckett
Hot Buttered Crab Dip

Jordan Bourke
Avocado Miso Dip with Dukkah

Chloe Coker & Jane Montgomery
Baba Ganoush
Herby Breadsticks
Paprika Pitta Chips
Sweet Potato Hummus

Ross Dobson
Muhammara
Spicy Chilli Bean Dip

Amy Ruth Finegold
Beetroot Herb Dip
Crostini
Flax-speckled Hummus with Kale
   Crisps
Light Aubergine Dip with Almond
   Chia Crackers
White Bean & Spinach Dip

Dunja Gulin
Mediterranean Tomato Hummus
Pea & Basil Hummus
Red Pepper & Buckwheat Crackers
Rye Crackers with Chia Seeds
Sesame Grissini
Spinach Hummus
Vegetable Crisps/Chips
Walnut & Red Pepper Hummus

Ursula Ferrigno
Lime Butter Dip with Lobster Tails
Saffron Lime Aioli with Asparagus

Matt Follas
Truffled Cauliflower Dip

Vicky Jones
Creamy Fava & Chicory Dip

Kathy Kordalis
Butter Bean Whip & Crudités Platter
Scorched Aubergine & Cauliflower Dip

Jenny Linford
Broad Bean & Ricotta Dip
Classic Hummus

Roast Garlic Herbed Labneh
Roasted Red Pepper Raita
Tomato Salsas

Dan May
Fresh Aïoli
Quick Chilli Lime Mayo
Roast Garlic & Chipotle Mayo
Wild Garlic and Chilli Pesto

Theo A. Michaels
Broad Bean 'Guacamole'
Red Pepper & Feta Dip
Remoulade Dip with Crab Fritters
Roasted Red Pepper & Chickpea
   Hummus
Taramasalata
Whipped Garlic Potato Dip

Hannah Miles
Bagel Toasts
Black Bean Dip with Blue Corn Chips
Blue Cheese and Walnut Dip
Cashew & Roasted Tomato Dip
French Onion Dip with Potato Chips
Hawaiian-style Bacon & Pineapple Dip
Homemade Classic Potato Chips
Hot Buffalo Chicken Wing Dip
Hot Philly Steak Dip
Layered 'Nacho' Dip
Maryland Crab Dip
Pea, Feta & Fresh Mint Dip
Peanut Satay Dip
Ranch Dip
Smoked Salmon, Horseradish & Dill
   Dip
Spicy Beer Mustard Dip with
   Maple-glazed Sausages
Warm Olive & Artichoke Dip

Louise Pickford
Blue Cheese Dip
Blue Cheese, Garlic & Thyme Dip with
   Potato Fries
Mont D'or Dip
Walnut Grissini

James Porter
Guacamame
Smoked 'ahi Dip

Fiona Smith
Artichoke Tarator
Macadamia & Chilli Dip

Milli Taylor
Beetroot Hummus
Creamy Artichoke & Spinach Dip
Cucumber & Mint Tzatziki
Roast Carrot, Ginger & Miso Dip
Romesco Dip with Grilled Spring
   Onions
Squid Ink Crackers

Jenna Zoe
Edamame & Wasabi Dip
Lighter Guacamole
Zesty Almond & Herb Pesto

Photography Credits

Jan Baldwin
Page 57

Peter Cassidy
Pages 14, 76, 127

Helen Cathcart
Pages 3, 7, 8, 82

Tara Fisher
Page 97

Richard Jung
Page 114

Mowie Kay
Pages 2, 4, 5, 13, 17, 22, 24, 26,
29, 30, 34, 36, 45, 49, 54, 58, 60,
66, 69, 70, 79, 89, 94, 98, 101, 108,
110, 113, 117, 118, 120, 122, 128,
130, 135, 138, 141, front and back
cover

Steve Painter
Page 85

William Reavell
Pages 12, 21, 63

Ian Wallace
Pages 33, 80, 106, 125

Claire Winfield
Pages 10, 39, 40, 46, 50, 53, 75,
86, 90, 93, 102, 105